Family History, Stories, and Other Lies

by

Roger M. Schlosser

DORRANCE PUBLISHING CO., INC.
PITTSBURGH, PENNSYLVANIA 15222

The events, people, and places herein are depicted to the best recollection of the author, who assumes complete and sole responsibility for the accuracy of this narrative.

ISBN: 978-1-4349-0752-3
Printed in the United States of America

First Printing

For information or to order additional books, please write:
Dorrance Publishing Co., Inc.
701 Smithfield St.
Pittsburgh, Pennsylvania 15222
U.S.A.
1-800-788-7654
www.dorrancebookstore.com

This work is dedicated
To me mather and her mather, my grandma,
And all the other Irish women in our family
Who made my brothers and me
"Irish."
And to my lovely wife
Who had to listen and watch much of it unfold
For nearly fifty years now—
She is the real Orange woman of my Irish life.
I sincerely hope that no one is offended by my telling
of these stories as I remember them in my imagination.
My intention is to entertain the reader as I have
been entertained by my imagination over
the years. If anyone is offended, I am
truly sorry about my imagination,
your sensitivities, and the rest
of the world's problems.

Contents

This is one of my favorite photos, taken in 1948; my mother is holding me, and I still remember the dress with the horses she would wear on "special" occasions.

Preface

This project is the product of years of experiences, remembrances, and creative imagination. Over the years, I have been able to tell and relive, to edit and enhance stories from my youth as they happened—well, as I remember the stories to have happened—okay, maybe as I wanted them to happen. So, in this work, I present stories as I imagine them to have happened. Anyone who knew my family in the early years might be able to discern the actual from the imagined or, put more crudely, fact from fiction. I am no longer able to. The years have played tricks on my memory, and my memory refuses to be simply a repository of facts. It is possible that I no longer remember every detail. That happens with age. But, what my mind cannot simply remember, it imagines. It fills in the blanks with likely happenings. That is to say it wants to be creative, to expand on and enhance the facts. That is not the same thing as lying exactly; it is expanding the stage, giving color to the setting, and bringing to life the events and characters of my youth. In short, my active mind is remembering my actually imagined experiences and is recreating the imagined actual stories.

Not that my youth was boring, but my Irish ancestors passed on to me both the gift of gab and a creative imagination to complement the stories. I imagine some of my Irish relations could tell great stories. Perhaps, they were "storytellers." If this is the case, and I can imagine it is the case, I am simply continuing the practice in a long line of storytellers. Over the years, my family, friends, and students have heard the stories of my youth. They would laugh and say, "That didn't really happen. Did it?" I would assure them that, in the good old days, anything was possible. I would often start out a story with, "Try to imagine…."

Several years ago, my mother was hospitalized because she had broken her hip and arm. Rehab took place in a nursing home where two of my former students were employed. They assured me they would look after her and help her with all they could. After about a week, they approached me and said they had asked my mom if any of the stories I had told them as students were true. Mom herself confirmed that, indeed, they were true. Both students confided that they had been somewhat skeptical as students, but now, they believed. Since then, many former and current students and friends have suggested that I record these stories. Some have encouraged me to write them down in book form. This volume is the product of their laughter at my experiences, remembrances, and creative imagination.

In some cases, I will go directly into the story announced in the title of the chapter. On other occasions, I will follow Bill Cosby's lead when he would say, "Okay, I told you that one, so I could tell you this one." I will introduce the actual subject of the chapter with a story or two that will set the stage or mood. These introductory tales will serve as an appetizer for the main course.

Although the chapters seem to ramble along in helter-skelter fashion, there is some method in my madness. The stream of consciousness patterns actually follows a logic within each chapter. As you follow along, see if you can sort out the connections within and between chapters. It is not so much a puzzle as a kaleidoscope. Some people's lives are puzzles, but mine is more of a rotating and tumbling kaleidoscope. So, as you peek in to my life, as I imagined it, the colors and shapes have tones and configurations that gave my world and life meaning, and I hope you can join me in reliving, as I imagine, parts of my life.

Introduction

Part One

As one can imagine, my profession as a teacher set the stage for my avocation of storytelling. I tried to relate the stories to the subject at hand as outlined in the course syllabus, but as is usually the case, students tended to get caught up and later to remember the stories rather than the actual subject under discussion. Try as I might, the questions focused on my illustrating and supporting story rather than the issue at hand. The stories were so natural for me to use as illustrations because I was so intimately familiar with them. They helped me help students understand, not simply know, the why behind the what of subjects.

The Irish side of my family seemed to relish in their stories, and I remember them from my earliest memories. These stories, most of which centered on the families that produced my immediate family, are natural building blocks for my illustrations in class.

There was one incident that stands out from my youth and was the event that sparked the storytelling. When I was young, my mother and my grandma would take one or two of us boys on a road-trip to Hartford, Michigan. Some of Grandma's ancestors settled there. We called on them once every year now, and they were gathered in the Hartford Cemetery, in the family plot.

Mom and Grandma would clean up the gravesites, occasionally stopping to rest. The weather was usually warm in late May as we prepared for Memorial Day by sprucing up the graves. Grandma would stop fussing, sit on the boarder of the plot, wipe her brow, and take a swig from the thermos bottle. Periodically, she would chat with other people visiting their loved ones at the cemetery, and they reminisced about the old days, catch up on who had done what, and who had died. These acquaintances had all the news and gossips from Hartford.

I believe this is photo was taken in Canada. It's of my Grandpa and Grandma Coffey with my mother, and her brother and sister, one of my uncles named Ted and an aunt, Mary Jane, whom I never knew.

From time to time, there was an elderly gentleman who was close by with his ancient mother who was also working on their family plot. He always came over to chat with Grandma. He knew all the old folks, was acquainted with all the old tales, and brought her up to date on somebody only people from Hartford would remember. He was a treasure trove of information about the area and the people. My grandma introduced me to him once. He was Willis Dunbar, a local celebrity. He was featured on the

Kalamazoo, Michigan, Channel 3 television station. He was also a distinguished professor of history at Western Michigan University and the author of the prestigious book *History of Michigan*. When I attended Western Michigan University, he was the chairperson of the History Department and was disappointed that I had chosen European history as my area of concentration instead of United States history, especially Michigan history, specifically local history. He suggested that I write down "all the stories that Emma Doyle, err Emma Coffey, knew and had told me." He was quite insistent on it. Now, this Emma Doyle was my grandma and his old flame. I only wish I had been more diligent with her's and mom's stories.

He knew that my grandma had told me all the stories when we were visiting Hartford on our annual pilgrimage when she was alive. She would clean around a particular grave and start the lessons. She and my mom, by simply being Irish, could turn a simply mundane biography into an epic story of migration, homesteading, and dynasty building, rivaling anything that the Greeks, Romans, or British authors ever devised.

She told of one particular Irish ancestor, a young girl named Kelly, if I'm not mistaken, who went down to Waterford to say good-bye to a neighboring family that had been evicted from their home and were immigrating to Canada. She came to the wharf with a basket of food to see them off. They said to her as she stood on the pier awaiting their departure, "Why stay? There is nothing for you here in Ireland. Come with us." As improbable as this sounded, and Grandma swore it was true, this sixteen-year-old girl, in a life-changing, instantaneous decision, jumped aboard the departing ship.

The first time I heard that story, I was thunderstruck. *Sweet Jesus,* I thought, *what a chance!* I wondered to myself, *What did her family say or do? Who told them what had happened? Did she ever see any of them again? Did she write and try to explain?* "Good grief," I muttered. Every time Grandma repeated that story for the benefit of a brother who was making the pilgrimage to the cemetery at Hartford for the first time, the credibility of the story never went down in my book. Rather, I could see it happening just so. My mom was like that ancient relative, and I imagined my grandmother was, too. All these Irish women I was related to were so strong.

Once, I asked my mom, "How did she do it? She didn't have a ticket. How'd she eat? Where did she stay on board?"

Mom said, "I'm glad you asked me and not Grandma. It's too hard for her to tell. But she confided in me once and never brought it up again. That young, innocent sixteen-year-old girl was taken in by the first mate. During the two-month voyage to Canada, she became his bunkmate. Do you understand? She had to give herself to him for her passage. That was how she got to Canada. She became his, well, sleeping mate. You understand?"

My mother, Kathyrn Mary Coffey, at about
four or five years of age.

I did, but it was beyond imagination. "She slept with him?"

Mom answered in a very hushed voice and in a tone of serious reverence, "Yes. That was the price for freedom."

"Did she marry him?" I asked.

"No," answered Mom, "after they landed in Canada, she was sold as an indentured servant to a family in Quebec. She had over six and a half years left of service."

I thought, *She certainly wasn't a whore or a prostitute, but what was she?* My mom read my face and my thoughts. Although I was probably eleven or twelve years old, I couldn't quite make it out. Mom said, "She was your great-great-grandma—a brave girl who had nothing but herself to offer for passage to a new life. Because of her, you, me, and Grandma are alive in America. She is a heroine to our family. We are all fortunate she had the courage of an Irish warrior. She gambled everything for a new life. You can be proud of her. She was great, and we are all related to her."

I was no longer baffled; Mom had set me straight. I have thought of that long-dead relative over the years and have thought that even if only a fragment of the story is true, what a fantastic story it still would be. What an incredible person. I was proud of my family. I wonder if other folks did that sort of thing, and it went unremembered. I was so happy that my family remembered these stories.

I asked what became of her in Canada. "Is that how part of the family ended up there?"

Grandma explained, "No. They came from another line."

"But what happened to her?" I asked.

"She was indentured for over six years there in Canada, like a slave, but she married an Irish newcomer. They wanted to come to the United States, but Irish folks were discriminated against, like Negro slaves were, back then," Grandma explained. "But it so happened that the St. Lawrence froze one winter. It doesn't happen very often. But this one year, it did, and the two of them braved it across the frozen St. Lawrence and got into upper New York State. The American Civil War, you know, the War Between the States, the North and the South, started up shortly after they came. The fellow she married joined the Union Army, replacing some United States citizens who'd been drafted. You could do that back then. He was in Sherman's Army and got himself killed outside of Atlanta, Georgia. By that time, there were two young boys in the family who had become without a dad. The Union Army, well, the United States Government, gave her a pension of a buckboard, two mules, and ten acres in Hartford, Michigan; that's how part of the family got to Hartford. She and those boys cleared the ten acres, and the stumps served as a fence for years."

"Gee, Grandma, it must have been hard," I added.

Grandma smiled and said, "That old woman didn't know hard. She did what she did because it had to be done. She and her boys had an orchard there, and you've seen it. Your mom has driven you by it. You've met Mildred Cronin, a neighbor still living next door to the old farmstead. The farm was finally sold some years back. Your Great-grandpa Doyle used to sit on the porch and yell at the Indians who would walk into town.

"They would yell, 'How, Ed Doyle.' There were a lot of Potowanamee. He'd yell at them to come up and get a cold drink of water. He was rough and sounded rough with them. But they liked him though. He'd yell to them, 'Hey, you damn old Indian. Get up here and get a drink. Nobody in town's going to give you one. Now, get the hell up here and get one.' They'd laugh and say, 'Okay, Ed Doyle.' Sometimes, when they would be going home, he'd call them up and give them a beer—never on the way into town, always on the way out. He didn't want them getting into any trouble. Hell, they could probably drink him under the table."

Grandma explained that Indians had helped during The Famine of the late 1840s in Ireland. "They sent corn when all the English did was feed the famine by sending nothing." She also explained that the English seemed to mistreat anyone whose nation began with an "I." "North American Indians, India's Indians, and the Irish," she explained. "The only folks that they like with the 'I' is themselves…as an Englishman 'I' want this and 'I' want that." It was her little joke, but she might have gotten it from Great-grandpa Ed Doyle. I would have liked to have known him in the flesh.

Grandma Coffey while holding me; taken in September of 1945. She had a "bit of the devil" in her which was passed on to her daughter, me, and my brothers, and speaking for myself, my own daughters and sons and my granddaughters and grandsons.

Although we were off the farm as it were, Grandma and Grandpa Coffey always had a big vegetable garden and, later, a fruit orchard just outside of Grand Rapids, Michigan. All of the grandkids would come out to the farm and pick apples and peaches. On breaks, we would sit around and hear family stories. Some were repeats, some were new. Grandpa even put in a new orchard and called it the grandkids' orchard and told about naming fields, tracks, trees, rock wells, and pools back in Ireland. They all had a story, and it was important to know these stories and to pass on these stories. The telling was as important as the stories Grandpa would explain. "The storyteller cultivated the story for the audience, and, depending on his talent, it would be a 'bountiful crop or a bust,'" Grandpa Coffey would explain. We never got to do much with the grandkids' orchard because he died in 1955, and Grandma sold the farm. Ironically, I now live about a mile and a half from it. It has been subdivided into a residential estate with apple trees in the backyards, dividing one lot from another. Whenever I drove by the old farm, I remember the stories and realize they were the real fruits that stayed with me.

I have my own small orchard in the back acre of my property now, and my grandkids romp through it as my brothers and cousins and I did through Grandpa's years ago. I have only about twenty apple trees. I've given one to each of the grandkids. They often want to go out and pick apples for their moms, my daughters. One time, I put a bunch of small matchbox cars under several trees for them to find. They went nuts. "Those trees grow matchbox cars," I explained. Another time, I put the small, individual size trick or treat Halloween candy bars out under other trees. They couldn't believe it. But seeing is believing. One other time, I placed about twenty-one-dollar bills under the trees. They really believed, if for only a short time, that "money grows on trees." They've started to catch on though. But in the process,

My grandfather Coffey's vegetable garden shortly after WWII in the Grand Rapids, just before he bought the apple orchard farm

new stories are beginning to emerge about their own "old" relatives. I am consciously cultivating a new set of family histories, stories, and legends for the new generation.

When my own kids were small, my wife and I would read to them each night before they went to sleep. Often, we read to them lying down in their beds. Sometimes, I would substitute a "story" for the reading. One of the favorites was "Rog and the Beanstalk," which goes as something like this:

Once, Grandma sent me up to the store to get milk, but I "talked to a stranger" who sold me some "magic beans." Grandma was angry because I "talked to a stranger," and I also didn't get the "milk." She tossed the beans out in the backyard and sent me to my room "for the rest of my life." In the morning, the beanstalk went all the way up into the clouds. I asked if I could climb it since, technically, I wouldn't be leaving the yard. Grandma said, "Okay, but be back for lunch." Up I went until I poked through the clouds. This giant had a magical chicken that he made lay golden eggs. When the giant went to the toilet, I grabbed the chicken and headed down the beanstalk. The giant gave chase, but I was yelling to Grandma to "get the ax." I handed the chicken to her and chopped down the vine with the giant still clinging to it about a mile up. When he fell, he made that hill by Grandma's house, and the chicken kept laying the golden eggs until she died, and then we ate her, but that was how we got the money to buy our house.

My kids would laugh and say, "Dad, that was 'Jack and the Beanstalk'—not 'Rog and the Beanstalk.'" I'd tell them they were mistaken and to ask Grandma the next time we saw her. She always smiled and winked at the kids and said, "Yep, that's right." They also learned of "Rog and the Billy Goats Gruff," and this is how it goes:

A bridge over a ravine on the way to the store where I once bought magical beans was the hideout of a big, old, mean troll. Uncle Gary had to go to the store one day, but, as he was crossing the bridge, his shoes made noise, and the mean old troll chased him off. He went and got Uncle Dick, but the two of them were no match for the mean old troll who chased them off again. They returned home and got Uncle Greg. The three made more racket crossing the bridge, and the troll violently chased them back home. Finally, they asked me for help. I led them to the bridge and told them to remove their shoes before they crossed. They quietly crossed, went to the store, and returned to the bridge. I told them to put their shoes on and to run across the bridge. As they did, so the mean old troll ran out to attack them, and I was waiting across the bridge from my brothers. He was concentrating on them, so I came up behind him and beat him to a pulp with a stick. He let out from the ravine with a yelp and was never seen again since.

"That's how I got to be a 'champion fighter,'" I would explain to the kids.

Again, they would laugh and say, "Dad, that's not how it went."

I would retort, "Ask Uncle Greg or Uncle Dick or Uncle Gary. See what they say." I'd lie, and they'd swear by it. Did I mention we are Irish?

My grandparents holding my mother

My grandparents with Grandpa Coffey, nearly forty years later, holding my grandpa kneeling with me

---

Part Two

My oldest grandson, John Edison Moore, was the funniest little kid when he was really young. Starting when he was about one year old, he had this infatuation with road-building and road-construction vehicles. One of his dad's younger sisters was dating and, eventually married, a fella who was working for a road construction company. This may have triggered his love for road builders and the equipment. He had every conceivable road construction toy imaginable. He knew their names and what they did, the whole package. He would use words that I didn't use until college. When he was about three years old, while we were driving along, he asked me about a building under construction.

He said, and, remember, he was about three years of age at the time, "I wonder, what sort of facility do you think they are building over there?" "Facility." At three, he wondered about "facilities."

We were driving by some new houses under construction a week or two later, and I asked him what kind of "facilities" he thought these examples were. He didn't answer right away, so I said I thought they were "living facilities." He just got this smirk on his face as if to say, "It's good that he is expanding his vocabulary."

But the road builders eventually gave way to hockey. At about three years of age, he would go into his folk's basement and swing either a child's golf club or a hockey stick and bat tennis balls or stuffed fake hockey pucks around the basement for hours. I remember going over there to visit them during the day and my daughter, Amy, saying that she had been down in the basement, playing goalie for hours. She would be exhausted and would ask me to play with him so she could rest. We told him we switched off at different periods. He never seemed to tire of whacking that stuffed puck or tennis ball.

It was about this same time he informed me that he would no longer call me "Bump Bump." He couldn't pronounce "grandpa," and it came out "Bump Bump." But by then, he was three years old, and he informed me one day, "Bump Bump, I'm not going to call you Bump Bump."

I thought, *Well, here it comes, grandpa.* But that was not the case.

Instead, he said, "I'm just going to call you Bump."

The name stuck; so, to all of my grandkids, I am "Bump," and my wife, Barb, is "Nana." In crowds, I do not have to listen up and inquire if the call "grandpa" is for me. My grandkids only call me, and I only answer to, "Bump." Many of their friends just call me "Bump." It's great, and I owe it all to my three-year-old grandson.

There was a "Bump" Eliott who coached the University of Michigan's football team back in the late '50s and early '60s. As I recall, he was a decent sort of guy; so, I had no issue with the name. In fact, I used to call John "Little Petie," or just "Petie." One day, my daughter, Amy, had John down at the college where I taught. After a short visit, she informed him that it was time to go, and she called him "John."

A colleague turned to me and said, "I thought his name was Petie. You always refer to him as Petie. Isn't his name Petie?"

I explained that his given name was "John," and that "Petie" was a nickname.

She asked, "Why Petie?" I explained that he had a little "Petie."

She was horrified, "He'll hate for it later."

I thought she might be right; so lately, I've taken to calling him "Hoss."

Part Three

With this background setting, it is time to identify and adorn the stage for the rest of the book. The setting is Grand Rapids, Michigan at first, then a suburb of Grand Rapids called Wyoming, Michigan later on. While renting an apartment on the west side of Grand Rapids, my folks bought a lot and started building a new house southwest of Grand Rapids. Everyone in the family, including my uncles and grandparents, especially my dad, worked on the new house in Wyoming, Michigan. The house was his pride and joy. It was built during the Korean War, and some building materials were scarce and expensive, but Dad managed. He kept the cost down by joining in on the construction. We all joined in on clearing the lot. Dad built a brick grill for cooking food, so no one would have to wander off in search of food. Wieners, hamburgers, and baked beans were the fare for most of the on-the-job meals.

The basement on our new house in Wyoming, Michigan, about the summer of 1950; you can see how secluded and rural the new house was out in Wyoming township, Michigan.

The lot was on a street that ran parallel to and one block west of Clyde Park Avenue. The new home site was on Burr Avenue. Burr was only a block long, and it ran between two streets: Floyd to the north and Bellevue on the south. Floyd and Bellevue ran off the main road to the east, Clyde Park Avenue, and dead-ended only a hundred yards beyond our street. So, our neighborhood was a square block, and the parish of Saint John Vianney owned the area inside the square block created by the four roads. Technically, it was owned by the Diocese of Grand Rapids, but the parishioners felt that the parish and all its buildings were theirs. It was our village. Our parents and grandparents worked on the parish, and, someday, we would work on the growing parish and contribute to its upkeep and additions. For the time being, my generation attended school, Sunday Mass, and served as altar boys at the church, convent, and for funerals at the cemetery. We knew the church land like our own yards and houses. We inherently assumed ownership. Saint John Vianney and the Village of Ars was ours. Our families were the past, the present, and the future of this place.

Winter 1950-51; snow on the grill in our backyard. It appears
in my memory and imagination that the snowfalls during my
youth were always massive when compared to later years.
This photo attests to one obvious reason for this impression: I
was so much smaller then. You can also see how thick the forest
was at the back of our house and why my mother was
constantly concerned with hunters mistaking one of us
for game. I am sure, even in the dead of winter,
I am wearing a red snowsuit.

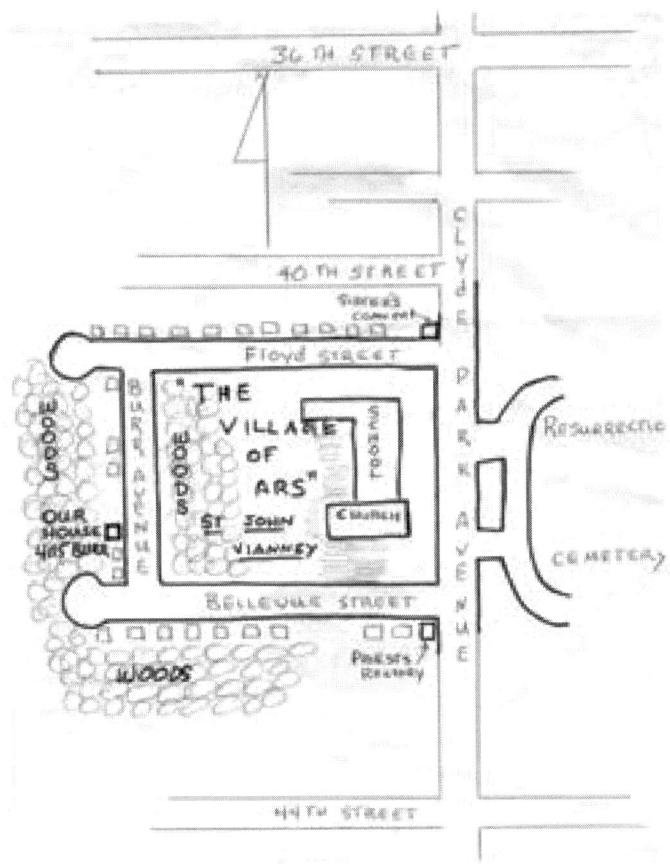

Saint John Vianney Catholic Parish and the Village of Ars

Saint John Vianney was a French priest, and he had been the curé of the Village of Ars in France a century and a half ago. The pastor of our Village of Ars was German as were the majority of parishioners whose houses circled the boundary and outer boundary of the parish grounds. Those houses were like bastions, and the families were like sentries protecting our Village of Ars. Better yet, the houses were like a medieval wall protecting our village.

The priest's rectory was built on the outer corner of Bellevue, and the school's sisters' convent was on the outer corner of Floyd. They were like the official guard houses protecting our "village."

Between the two sentinels on the inside of the block were the church, school, playground, and sports fields. Across from the rectory, church, school, and convent ran Resurrection Cemetery for a quarter of a mile. The Village of Ars was isolated, parochial, and a private enclave. Everyone knew everyone, there were no secrets, and everyone was there for you in your time of need. It was a wonderful place to live and grow up in or, possibly, return to when the time came. Some of my fondest memories to this day are set in that square block and the adjacent area.

We lived on the "backstreet" as it were, along the western boundary to this village and across from the rear of the church, school, and the grounds. Across the street from our house and at the rear of the church's property was the wooded area that served as a buffer to all the doings at the church and the school. Over the years, the woods would be thinned out and become more of a park. But in the early days, it was lush, and a safe, if not private, place to play. Almost all the kids played in the schoolyard or in the church woods.

In the early days, the whole setting of the Village of Ars was out in the country. Our village was physically out in the country in those days with woods and fields to the rear of our houses and to the south, all the way to the next main road, 44th Street, half a mile away. Hunters prowled the area for pheasants and deer, and my mother always dressed us in bright red for a couple of months in the fall as a precaution. The "village" square block was the safest place for the kids of our neighborhood to play. My brothers and I were so loud that there wasn't any game for miles I'm sure, but it put my mom's mind to rest, knowing she had decked us out in hunter's red. To the many Eastern European DPs (displaced persons) who were relocating in the environs, we must have looked like young communist pioneers. My mom could never figure out why they avoided us. In hindsight, I eventually figured it out.

Part Four

Although our "village" was a tight community with several families related to one another, there was a general acceptance of newcomers who brought new ideas, experiences, and practices, among other things, to the neighborhood. To cite just one example, let me introduce a family who had an immediate impact back then and which has persevered right to the present. This family supplied my mom with her best friend for forty odd years, and her husband was a friend of my dad's. I learned some "broken" French from them; a kid from three doors down from our house married the oldest daughter, their only son became one of my brother's best friends, and their youngest daughter became the "little sister" my brothers and I never had.

The new family moved just around the corner on Bellevue, and they were French-Canadians, the Des Pres family. Everyone in the neighborhood was thrilled because we finally had someone who was French, living in the Village of Ars and the parish of Saint John Vianney. Furthermore, they understood hockey. They had relatives back up in Canada and could get hockey sticks and pucks. I mean real hockey pucks. We would no longer have to use weighted tuna fish cans sealed with electrical tape.

The whole family knew how to skate. The village kids built a hockey rink across the street from their house. It was like a frozen holy water or baptismal fount in their honor. Fred, the dad, had real hockey skates, and his wife, Jeanette, and their daughter would glide around the rink with such grace that we hated to interrupt them with our stupid attempts at hockey. We often just stood there, or tried to stand up on the ice, and watched them. Everyone knew these people were a good addition to the neighborhood, and we were lucky to have them, and their kids: Dianne, Mark, and Karen.

Jeanette was about my mom's age, and she spoke English with an accent, a French-Canadian accent. We all began saying "Hey" at the end of each sentence. Her accent and pronunciation were contagious. She became another aunt, or "Tante," to all of us Schlosser boys. She constantly referred to herself as a "JC," which we thought meant some religious affiliation or lay order, like "Jesus Christ," or "Jesus' Comrade," or "Joyous Christian," or something like that.

We discussed it over meals for about a week or two. Then, my mom just asked Jeanette, "What does that 'JC' actually mean?" She used it in some peculiar ways and, at times, in a strange context. Jeanette looked at us like we were weird. She said, "Just a come." You know, she was from Saulte Ste. Marie, Canada, and she was a "just a come" to the United States. She was a "JC." We all went around saying we were all "JCs, hey."

I don't know if Jeanette introduced my mother to wine, but she, sure as hell, encouraged her in drinking it pretty regularly. My brother, Gary, likes to recall the time he came home from school to find Jeanette and mom sitting in the bathtub with two glasses and an empty bottle of wine. They had planned to wall-paper the bathroom shortly after all of us boys headed off to school. They were still working at it at lunchtime. But, three hours later, they had run out of paper, for some reason settled in the tub, opened the wine, and drained the bottle. We found out later that they had finished off an opened one from the day before, also.

There they were, in the bathtub, paper remnants and glue stuck to them. They were laughing and giggling, and became all the more helpless as more and more of us came home to see this sight. Mom said they were "resting." They decided to sit in the tub on their break because they had all the glue sticking to them, and, if they fell, they wouldn't fall far, and the tub would help to support them. Jeanette knew she had to get home because her son had gone home from school, too. The problem was the two of them could not get out of the tub. They were stuck, not from the paste or glue, but, in large part, from the wine.

We went and got her son, and he stayed at our house until they eventually got out of the tub. We had also gone and gotten some of our friends to come and see what was going on in our bathroom. I can still hear the two perfectly-dry bathing beauties saying, "Oh my God, look who they have here now." Then, they would start laughing and be rendered helpless again. I think it was about four-thirty in the afternoon before they finally got out of that tub. The whole neighborhood heard about the incident within a day or two, and it became part of the "Jeanette-Kay" lore. Everyone in the neighborhood thought it was funny, except for Jeanette's husband and my dad.

Jeanette taught us some French words and phrases. When I took the first year of my master's degree in Europe, I traveled to France over the Christmas break. I took a train from London to Dover, caught the ferry to Calais, and then cashed in my Euro-rail Pass to Paris. I got in about three-thirty in the afternoon on a dark day in December. I had a suitcase and a shoulder bag with all that I would need for about a month.

I got off the train at Gare du Nord, found the Metro I needed at Gare de l'Est, and crossed the Seine River for the Left Bank. I had Frommers's *Europe on Five Dollars a Day* and was looking for a cheap hotel on the Rue Cluny. It was located just beyond the ruins of a monastery by the same name. I was seeking number 114. The street only ran one block and dead-ended into a building. The last number on the street was 54. I was lost.

I went back out to the main street and double-checked the street name. It was correct. There was a vendor selling long, skinny hot dogs from a wagon. I hadn't had anything to eat since the day before, and I was famished. So, I took out ten francs and bought two of the dogs. He cut two lengths of French bread and jammed them on a spike-like object. He mumbled something, which I took to mean, "Do you want mustard?" I nodded my head indicating "yes." He handed the two-foot long hot dogs to me but failed to give me my change.

At first, I stood there patiently, but then, started to gesture that I expected about six francs change. He waited on other customers and ignored me. I called him every vulgar name I could think of and used several choice adjectives. I even managed a few French beauties which were difficult for him and the passers-by to ignore. I eventually felt that getting screwed out of one dollar and twenty cents wasn't worth the hassle. I returned to the Rue Cluny, hoping that the building obstructing my way to number 114 had moved.

It hadn't. I walked to the end of the street, checked the book again, set my bags down, and bit into my expensive supper only to nearly gag to death on the mustard. Damn, it was not only hot; it took my breath away. Tears came to my eyes. Breathing hurt, my mouth was on fire, and I overpaid for this crap. It was then that I noticed a guy was up a ladder painting a sign over a shop front.

I said, "Pardon monsieur, number 114?" He was holding his brush in one hand and the pail of paint in the other, balancing ever so gently on the third rung from the top. He motioned that the street began on the other side of the building, and that 114 was in fact over there. I was grateful, and, as I picked up my bags to divert around the building, I started to thank him in my best lingua franqua. What I wanted to say was, "*Merci beaucoup*." But what I heard myself saying was, "*Merci grosse fesse*," which is not "thanks very much," but "thanks fat ass." I heard these words come out of my mouth. I couldn't believe it. It was like an out-of-body experience. I was thinking one thing and saying something quite different. The guy was teetering at the top of the ladder with this disgusted look on his face.

I said, "No, no, pardon, pardon. *Merci beaucoup*." I hurried away before it dawned on him to "accidentally" drop the bucket of paint on me. That's all I would have needed to start and end my first day in Paris. I eventually found number 114, checked in for about five days, and had a good time touring Paris. I could not wait to get home and tell Jeanette my first attempt to communicate to the French in the French she had taught me. She laughed and laughed when I did return home and related my experience to her.

Several years later, the elder Des Pres and my parents joined a college-run tour of France I was leading. They reveled in reliving the story of my first trip to Paris as I took them to all the spots where I had been humiliated. The best part came after several days in Paris when Jeanette admitted she couldn't understand the Parisians at all. She said, "They don't speak my kind of French."

Part Five

Well, not to get too far ahead of myself and to get back to the start of the story, let's return to the 1950s, on the west side of Grand Rapids, and then to the Village of Ars out in Wyoming. The neighborhood was, in spite of our dressing like young communist pioneers for months at a time and scaring some of the "JCs," quite tight, like any small community. There were few secrets, and everyone knew everybody pretty well. I could play hooky from school and be a half a mile away down near 36th Street or Burlingame, and people would yell out my name from a passing car or house and ask why I wasn't in school. They'd say, "Get back to school, or I'll tell your mom." I went straight away because I didn't want to deal with my mom concerning any infraction of the rules.

An assistant priest at the parish used to come by after supper to pay a call. He taught my brothers and me to play Black Jack while he had a drink of the hard stuff. He would come once a week, play a friendly game of cards, and polish off about half a bottle. I would walk him back up to the rectory at the end of the game. He once explained that "most of the rules, regulations, practices, and beliefs of the Church were BS and just some old pope's, cardinal's, and bishop's beliefs." I mulled that over for years, and I must say it helped me take much of the stuff of the Church with a grain of salt. Father P. was one honest priest. He is probably the reason I stayed Catholic back then and even now.

Chapter One

Me Mather, Kathyrn Mary Schlosser, née Coffey

My dad's family was German, from the Coblenz area. After World War II, Dad took a job with a Swiss pharmaceutical company. Among other things, they were clean, efficient, punctual, and all was in order. At certain times of the year, Dad was only home one week out of the month, so my Irish mother, Katie [nee O'Coffey], had my brothers and me all to herself. Actually, that makes it sound much more romantic than it was. The fact was that she was stuck with us, and since we did not know any better and she was our mom, it wasn't so much that we we're stuck with her as there we all were, except for my dad, out there on the edge of the town, trying each other's nerves.

Mom's family was Irish. Her mother's family came from Wicklow, in the south of Ireland, and her father's people were from "the north" of Ireland. Mom was clean, and she kept us clean, "Irish clean," a little Irish lace, that is cobwebs, and some banshee dust, which was plain old dust. She was more or less efficient, considering she was Irish. Getting something done without too much fuss was the plan. There was punctuality, and there was "Irish time," and she and we went by the latter. There were bits of time as there were bits of anything, and to be early or late a bit was just fine. What exactly a bit was could not be defined. It was dependent on who was late or early. A somebody was excused. A nobody was condemned. There certainly was an order to reality, and she made us very aware of it, as I will explain later. She was the "mather," and we were her brood. She ruled the roost, and we all loved her for it. Never in our whole lives could we, or would we, ever envision it any other way.

My mom in the mid-'30s as a Catholic Central Junior or Senior

As a matter of fact, there were nine boys born to Kathyrn Mary Schlosser née Coffey, and, although only four saw their twentieth birthday, my dad used to say he had his own baseball team. We lived in a rather large ranch-style house out in Wyoming, Michigan, a suburb of Grand Rapids, Michigan. There was one bathroom, a large living room, and several bedrooms. The bedrooms were like dark caverns, the drapes usually drawn for privacy (no one lived next door to us for nearly twenty years, so I never really knew who might be infringing on our privacy), but, in fact, there was no privacy with all of us boys in this house and only one bathroom. It was like living in a gold fish bowl most of the time.

When Dad was gone, my mom took a page out of *Stalag 17*, a novel about the famous prisoner of war camp ran by the Germans during World War II, because she ran the house like a prison camp. There were more or less exact times for everything: when we ate, washed for meals and before bed, and retired to the cave to sleep. It happened when she said it was going to happen, and you'd pretty damn well had better been paying attention when she decided the exact times for the happenings. The times might vary, but the time decided upon was exact. This routine was sacred. It seldom, if ever, was altered. It had been established a long time back in Ireland or by the Pope—I can't remember which. I remember she told us all once, and we believed her.

One might wonder about things Mom said, but you never questioned her, certainly never to her face and never in front of anyone else. It simply wasn't done. How did she put it? "I'll knock you into the middle of next week," or was it, "I'll hit you so you won't know if you're foot or horseback." When my mom gave such warnings, they had the authority of God's anointed. She was like a woman priest, a female bishop. Hell, her middle name was "Mary." So, obviously, she was somehow associated with, if not distantly related to, Christ's very mother. If you didn't believe that, all you had to do was ask her, "Mom, were you named after Jesus' mom or something?"

Her stare would go right through you. Then, she would say, "Who in Sam Hill do you think you are even asking such a question?" At the time, we interpreted her answer as affirming the obvious: her "close" relationship with the Virgin Mary and the audacity to even question it. It never entered our mind that her question might relate to the incredulous physical and theological impossibility of a relationship between her and the Virgin. No one laughed, and, deep down in our collective consciousness, we all knew that the guilty son who had asked such a presumptuous question could depend on the fact that she would never stand at the foot of the cross that obviously awaited him sooner than later.

Back in the cave we called our bedroom, under the cover of darkness and the quiet of night, one of her prodigal sons once suggested Christ's mom was actually named after our mom, "Katie," but the Virgin changed it to Mom's middle name "Mary" because Mom would never turn the cheek and humbly take her son's crucifixion in such a resigned way. Although our mom wasn't that old, she had been through the mill and was Irish and wouldn't take any crap from the Romans, Jews, the English, or anyone. She simply wouldn't take crap from anybody. She was Irish. I remember her telling us one time that, since we were Catholic, that is the oldest form and genuine Christians, we might have to endure insults from time to time at the hands of pagans, schismatics, heretics, and heathens. And we might have to turn the cheek if assaulted for our religious beliefs. "But then, boys, remember you're Irish and beat the hell out of them." The way she explained it was like a new commandment, and not to perform accordingly was tantamount to a sin.

But in the privacy of our bedroom, we all giggled and choked the laughs back, and trembled for fear that she would come in to find out what was going on. After a few moments of quiet, the silence would be broken by a voice from the darkness asking, "Who the hell is Sam Hill?" The tortuous, muffled laughing would erupt again and only quieted out of fear.

We feared her and loved her, and our love for her was in part based on fear. Don't get me wrong; we sincerely loved her for just being our mom, for all she did for us, and, even back then, we were conscious of the fact that she did a lot. With my dad gone so much, she was up well before we got up in the morning, getting our breakfast and doing chores, and she was still doing housework well after we went to bed at night. She was certainly a saint. And just as you feared the wrath of a just God, and feared the condemnation of His holy saints, so we feared this saint among us, our mother. And like some of the prophets of the Old Testament who railed against evil and injustice, she could and would do the same...her voice, her anger, her demeanor, and her presence was intimidating. And, like some figure from the Old Testament, she had that righteous anger. In fact, it seemed that she wasn't happy unless she was "pissed" at something or somebody.

Being "pissed" (she never used the word, after all, she was a "lady" as she used to say with a laugh) was always translated as "getting her Irish up" over something or somebody. Now, this was serious stuff. She could explain political events within this context: When President Kennedy "got his Irish up" and the "fat little Russian (Ukrainian) Khrushchev backed down," she would remind us. You get your Irish up, and anything is possible. She could put it within a sports context: The reason Notre Dame's Fighting Irish weren't winning football games in the late 1950s and early '60s was that they "didn't get their Irish up, and that's a sin." Losses were not simply losses; they were a sin to boot. Whew, she was right, shewas always right, and she was always

Mother and child: Mom holding me in the fall of 1945.

able to put things like her analysis and conclusions in a theological context: it was a "sin."

She could put almost anything in a religious context. It was a "sin." She could spot sin in simply failing to perform well. Like all great prophets and saints, she knew it when she saw it. What to the rest of the world was a screw up, bad luck, or simply performing poorly, she saw it as a serious flaw, a breach of a sacred covenant, a sin in most cases. Taking this into account, we all knew who she was since she spoke with authority, divinely inspired authority. Well, she and you know who were somehow related; both having the name Mary was no coincidence. Of that we were sure.

Being Irish, she knew sin and sinners when she encountered them. She was never one to back down in holding her condemnation in or to sacrifice principles for expediency or etiquette. Sometimes, this could be very embarrassing, not to her, but for me. I was teaching at a college in Grand Rapids, and, every year, I led study tours to Europe. We went to England and Ireland one year. The recent "troubles" in the north of Ireland were in full swing, and I thought it would be timely to go to the United Kingdom and the Republic of Ireland to hear both the official and unofficial comments. I had some contacts in both governments that we utilized as well as the man and woman in the streets. It was a huge success. I provided students with articles and extracts of books that put the Anglo-Irish problem in perspective with an historical overview.

Before we left London for Dublin, I scheduled a stop out at Windsor Castle for the group. Saint George's Chapel is an architectural gem of the late-English gothic style.

As I was walking the group through the chapel, a group that happened to include my mother, I stopped mid-way down the central isle, drew back the carpet revealing an engraved stone marking the tomb of one of England's famous monarchs. I asked if anyone in the group knew who was buried here as opposed to the more famous and traditional resting place of English monarchs, Westminster Abbey? There was universal silence. I pointed out and voiced the inscription, "Henricus Rex VIII."

Again, there was silence, but finally, "Henry. King Henry, the eighth?"

Before I could answer, "Right," my mother said, "Henry, The Sinner."

Besides my group of about twenty, other visitors were gathered around. To my amazement and horror, me Irish Mather Katie O'Coffey hissed the name "Sasanach," the Irish name for the English. Then, she hawked up from deep in her throat a knot of whatever and spit it contemptuously on the grave and walked out of the church. My students did not shrink from the outrageous behavior of my mom. They rather enjoyed it, being enlightened of her stance about the United Kingdom from earlier comments I had made about her in class and her recent opinions expressed on the tour itself. The only place she wanted to visit in London had been the site of Saint Thomas More's estate in Chelsea, along the River Thames. Saint Thomas More, if you will recall, was executed by Henry VIII in 1535 for remaining a Roman Catholic and all that it entailed in the sixteenth century in Britain. Mom's antics at Windsor were the statements and actions of an Irish Catholic punctuating her feelings about the Brits based on typical Irish tradition accentuated by the recent "troubles."

I remember that 1954 was designated a Marian Year by the Catholic Church, a full year of special commemoration to the mother of Christ for Catholics around the globe. Remembering the association of The Virgin Mary and my mom, Kathyrn Mary, it took on a special importance for our family. It so happened that an assistant priest in our parish was from Ireland, and he had a special attachment to our family, being headed by me Irish Mather. I specifically remember him coming over to the house one day and telling my mom that Protestant Orangemen had attacked a Catholic procession at Portadown on the way from the north of Ireland to the Republic for some event concerning the Marian Year. She was incensed, and her hatred for the British puppet, sham, statelet of "Northern Ireland," and all its supportive organizations such as the Orange Order, the Royal Ulster Constabulary, the police auxiliaries, the B-Specials, and the all Brits in general, was heightened or deepened or whatever to levels inexperienced by anyone in our family up to that point. Only the

"Bloody Sunday" massacre, in January of 1972, of peaceful, un-armed citizens in Derry by British Paratroops matched the fe-rocity of her 1954 hatred and disgust of "them."

About a year after the Portadown attack, my mom said, "Some clown named Brian Faulkner led an Orange parade through a Catholic area in a show of triumphalism." My mom wanted to go to Chicago to burn a Union Jack outside the British consulate. She also explained she would "like to tap that S.O.B. with an ax." My dad came home in time to prevent her from going off to Chicago or the north of Ireland.

You can imagine that all these episodes awakened in her and, increasingly, in her sons the roots of our Irish and Fenian her-itage. As she explained more than once to us, "It's neither your name nor the fact that your parents are Irish that makes you Irish, real Irish, really Irish." Everyone who is Irish has something Irish flowing through their veins, is part of the matter of their bones and flesh; it's encoded deep in their brains, and is subliminally present in their memory. All one has to do is to recognize this and act accordingly. Uncover and recover your Irish memory and being. And nothing sparks this process better than British arro-gance, ignorance, and atrocities. "Leave it to the Brits," Mom used to say. "They bring out the Irish in the Irish by their crimes against us."

Mom had her own rendition of *Gone with the Wind's* story of having lost uncles during the war. Mom's uncles, Seamus and Sean, were also killed by the British during the war. She told us boys the name of the battle, but it wasn't until I was in high school that I came home after school one day and asked her specifically about it. "Mom, did you say it was the Battle of Bastogne?"

"No," she replied.

"The Battle of Britain?"

"No."

"The Battle of Bologna?"

"No," she said again. Then, she asserted, "It was the Battle of the Boyne."

I said, "The Battle of the Boyne was over three hundred years ago. You gave me the impression you knew those uncles, had played with them, and that they had given you horsy rides on the shins." She said one of the most profound things I ever heard and what she said helped me understand a lot of history.

She said, "Never let time stand in the way of history. The British killed my uncles, and they were your uncles, too—*your* uncles, Seamus and Sean. It was tragic. It's just that simple." This may sound suspiciously like some story taken out of *Gone with the Wind*, but, I assure you, she claimed it was true, and she repeated the story with such conviction that my brothers and I all "believed."

When my brothers and I were young, we really didn't get all of what she was saying and implying. But, over the years, it began to sink in. Overtime, I found myself telling my kids about those uncles, and now, I tell my grandkids about those two uncles who were killed by the Brits. Over the years, it's been apparent what she told us was not wasted. Much of it has become our lore. It is just that simple.

Chapter Two

The Bite of the Swing

All of this leads me to the topic of the "bite" and the "swing." At this time, our family was living on the west side of Grand Rapids, Michigan, next to St. James Parish and School on Bridge Street. I still get reminders of my youth on the west side. The old Polish *bushas* would make toast every morning by laying the slice of bread in the oven, and they would leave the door of the oven open to heat up the kitchen and keep an eye on the toast. It always burned and gave off an aroma that was very distinct. I smell it still once in a while, and I am mentally transported back sixty years to growing up on the west side.

The kids who lived downstairs from us would put me in a wagon, and we would go about four blocks away to a bakery for pumpernickel bread once a week. It was a dangerous trip because there were houses of tough Polish kids who would rush out and assault us. Usually, it was only verbal, but, occasionally, it turned out to be a shove, a spit, or a slug. I was just along for the ride, so the Schmidt kids, who were a year or two older than me, took the brunt of the encounter. Actually, I do not remember ever getting roughed up or spat upon. But I vividly recall the other two having problems.

We would be going along Stocking Street, and Tommy would say to me, "Hold on, some mean kids live right up here, and we are going to race past them." His sister, Marilyn, would run alongside with a look of terror on her face. When we made it past the house, there was instant relief. When we were intercepted, there was hell to pay for the two of them. There were two houses that spelled trouble. Seldom would we get by both. If we did, the good news was we were halfway through the trip, and the bad news was that we were only halfway through. We would get the bread, but we had to return home the same way. They knew we had to come back, and they waited for us. Tom and Marilyn would run like crazy, and I'd bump along in the wagon.

I never understood why those kids hassled us. Was it because we weren't Polish, or was it because they went to a different school or church, or did they do it just for fun? The west side was a mysterious place because it often defied reason, had no logic, and sounded foreign. The Schmidts downstairs and my family were the only two who spoke English at home. The rest were Polish, Lithuanian, or Latvian. Many houses had old *bushas* who would stand around at midday and jabber in their own language. Each nationality had their own parish or church. The Latvians had a Protestant Church about four blocks away, near the German Parish of Saint Mary. The Poles had the huge church of Saint Adalbert, and the Lithuanians had Saints Peter and Paul. There was an Irish parish right behind our home called Saint James.

My mom had a habit of getting pregnant while we lived on the west side. The Schmidt kids were sure it was the pumpernickel bread. Be that as it may, the old *bushas* would say in their broken English, "I see the stork circling your house. It won't be long now." I would ask my mom what they were talking about. I knew I was expecting a baby brother or sister, but I had always heard about it falling off a "cabbage truck" or being found in a "potato patch." Mom would explain that these people were from Eastern Europe; they were "DPs" (Displaced Persons), and they did things differently there.

My mom in her senior year at Grand Rapids Catholic Central High School. When her little brother, my uncle, Ted Coffey, got in scrapes in high school during baseball games where he excelled as a pitcher, being drafted by the Brooklyn Dodgers, she would wade into the donnybrook and hold her own against the "boys" from rival Creston High School.

The old *bushas* would have the ragman come once a week with his large push wagon. He spoke no English and ignored us kids entirely. But the iceman was another story altogether. Virtually, every *busha* had an icebox on the back stoop or porch. When the iceman came each week, the kids would wait for him and beg him to chip a piece or two of ice off the block he was delivering so we could suck it. If the *bushas* caught us begging, they would shoo us away with a broom. If a *busha* caught an iceman chipping us some ice, she yelled at him until he was out of sight. No one knew what she was saying, but she was angry. He had probably given us twenty minutes worth of ice from her icebox this next week. And indeed, the next week, she'd be waiting for him and us with a broom in hand.

My dad bought the first television in the block. Each night, my folks would invite a different family to watch an hour or two of TV. There were three channels as I recall, and they were only on for about four hours a day. The *Howdy Doody* show was the kids' favorite. We were lined up in front of the TV and were as quite as if we were in the movie house. My family was considered rich by the locals because we had the TV, an electric stove, and refrigerator. I suppose we were, in most ways. The west side was working class, and the men worked in the famous furniture factories of Grand Rapids.

I went to kindergarten at Stocking School where I met guys I would run into again in high school. And it was in kindergarten that I first played hooky from school. My mom had just had another baby, and she was bringing him home from the hospital. Grandma Coffey was at the apartment waiting for the joyous event, and I was not going to miss it either. At recess, I hid in the bushes, and, when everyone went in at the bell, off I went for home to welcome my brother and my mom. Grandma Coffey was waiting for me, having gotten a call from school, and she vacillated between a frown and a grin as we both awaited the glorious arrival.

When my folks arrived with my newest little brother, I don't recall what my dad said, but I'm sure it was something to the effect that I couldn't run away from school again. I do remember my mom's reaction at first. Eventually, she said, "We shouldn't have sent you to school today. It was too important a day, wasn't it?" I remember she grinned at me and hugged me. When I think of that moment, even after all these years, I can still feel how good it felt. It was better than ice cream or a toy.

It was about a year before were moved out to the suburb of Wyoming. I was in kindergarten at a local public school as I mentioned earlier since the Catholic grade school right next door was bulging at the seams and couldn't find space for a kindergarten. But I would crawl through the fence into the St. James playground, and I would utilize their swings. These were real playground swings, tall, thick chain-link dropping from the high cross pole, and attached to the seat. You could get arch, velocity, and height. This was the real thing. I loved it.

One day, as I was swinging, some big kid I had never seen before came up and grabbed the chain of the swing I was on. I jerked violently from side to side. The Schmidt kids from downstairs had the other two workable swings. They just watched and didn't say a thing, not wanting to draw the attention of the bully to them. I didn't blame them for not coming to my aid. He was bigger than any of us, and he was focused on me so they just kept swinging. They were the ones who caught grief when we went for pumpernickel, and I never got it then. So, fair was fair.

The fourth swing was broken. I was the smallest kid, so I was the target for the tough who prized a swing, my swing. I slowed down and straightened out, and the bully tried to jerk me off the swing. I had a death grip on the chains. Before I knew what was happening, he bit me on the arm, right on the forearm. I screamed, let go of the chains, slid off the seat, and ran for home in pain.

Mom obviously heard me coming, and she bent down and grabbed me by the shoulders and asked what I was screaming about.

I showed her my forearm with the teeth marks, some of them with blood surfacing. When I saw the blood, the wound hurt all that much more, and I winced, exhaled, and waited for my mother's comfort.

Holding my arm tenderly now, she inquired how and why it happened.

In my most convincing voice, I described the attack and positioned myself as the pathetic victim. I was ready for tender loving care. But what happened next was incredible. She stood up and said, "What did you do to him?"

"Mom, I was just swinging, and he bit me. I wasn't...." I never finished the statement. I had totally misunderstood the question.

She understood that I was innocent and a victim. What she wanted to know was what I did *then* to the kid in retaliation for his attack. She asked, "What did you do to him for biting you?"

"I ran home to you," I said.

"So, you didn't do anything to him for what he did?" she asked incredulously.

I could only manage a pathetic, "No."

She stood up straight and said, "You go back over there and get that swing back or I'll bite that arm damned near off."

I was moving like I was possessed because my mom was perfectly capable of doing anything she threatened to do.

I don't know if the kid saw me coming or not. I was on him like a rabid dog. I bit him any place my mouth landed. I was possessed. I bit him on the forearm, bicep, cheek, and nose. He fell off the swing, "my swing," exposing the back of his head, his neck, and his shoulders. As he tried to fight me off, I got the back of his arm, his back and one side, his butt and legs. He shrieked and finally broke free, running for his life. I didn't give chase. I savored the taste of victory. It had been as if I was "righteously" possessed. I was hungry, if not for justice, then certainly for retribution and absolution from my mother. I was no longer scared because I had to go back to her. Now, I was confident and righteous, and I quite possibly had the taste of blood in my mouth. I can imagine it was dripping from my lips and teeth, my shirt covered in the evidence of retribution. I could face her now as a proud son. I was also sure she would be proud of her "son."

She was waiting in the backyard near the hole in the fence I used to enter the playground. Apparently, the blood had dripped off my face and rubbed off my shirt because all she did was nod in approval and started up the stairs to the second floor. But as she turned, I saw a smile cross her face. I never said what I *then* did, but she knew. Did she watch through the fence? I never asked then or later because events again took over. All the same, she knew, and she knew the older kids from downstairs also knew and understood what she expected and what I was capable of doing if I was a victim of any injustice. They were nice kids to me, but Mom always figured it was necessary to demonstrate to friend or foe what was in store for betrayal. They were German-Irish, as were we, so Mom said they would understand. No harm was meant because no harm would ever come from them. They were like us, not the Poles, Latvians, and Lithuanians that surrounded us on Grand Rapids' west side.

Me on a swing in our Wyoming backyard,
along with my two brothers

Justice had been done; I had learned I could hold my own against older and bigger kids, and the neighbor kids had also seen a side of me that they had not witnessed before. What a day, lessons had been learned all around. And, just then, my dad showed up. Boy, this was great. Just as we were starting up the stairs around the corner came the bitten bully kid, and, obviously, his mom. The kid looked miserable; he was definitely in pain, and I had caused it. His mother was irate, and she glared at me. Then, she started screaming that I should be chained to a tree, be brought to the dog pound, get rabies shots, and have a muzzle fitted. Then, she pulled her kid out from behind her and displayed his wounds.

My dad, who knew nothing of the incident, just stood there in amazement. His mouth was open in disbelief. The little circle eventually ended up with my dad next to the bully's mom, me next to my dad, and the bully, a full head taller than me, standing close to me. My mom had slid out of the circle and stood behind my dad and the bully's mom, and as the bully's mother described the placement, the depth, and the broken skin on her son's body in great detail, my mother, just out of everyone's sight but mine, mimicked clapping at each gory aspect, nodding her head and grinning from ear to ear. My dad was scowling and shaking his head from side to side and beginning to grimace as the bully moaned. But, there she was, my mother, observable only to myself, enjoying every minute of it; so proud of the damage I had caused, the pain I had inflicted, the reputation I had cultivated this day with the bully and his family, the neighborhood kids (and those they told about the incident), and the family and friends she would share this with. She was so proud just as my dad was becoming so disturbed and disgusted by it all.

This is a picture of me about the time I was becoming
a self-righteous fighter for my rights and taking
my first firearms lessons.

Mixed messages, you might imagine? Not so. Dad was a frequent visitor to the family, but Mom was the law. She ruled. All of us were pawns on her chessboard and in her game. There was no confusion. It was perfectly clear. Dad was out of the loop, an occasional player, and certainly not in the same league as was Mom. She called the shots, and her word (even silent words and gestures) was the law.

Mom's law was the highest, but it was not the only law I knew of growing up in the west side. Two older guys lived on each side of our apartment. They were in high school and coleaders of a "gang." The gangs ran the west side of Grand Rapids, and their word was the law, too.

"Dave" lived to the south of our place, on the second floor. We could look across and into his apartment. Our mothers were friends. They had a flat roof off the back of their place, and it was used by the gang. It overlooked an ally where garages stored bags of grain for a local bakery.

About the time of my first firearms lesson in the west side of
Grand Rapids in 1950

The gang made "zip guns" out of car aerials which held twenty-two shells. They shot at the rats and pigeons around the garage. I was allowed to go up there by my mom, and "Rick" and the other guy, "Bob," took care of me. I was in kindergarten. I shot my first gun off that roof. I shot at a rat with a homemade zip gun.

"Dave" and "Bob" said I was "okay" because of what I had done to the bully over the swing. They patted me on the head and said, "Bull Dog, you're okay." Mom was correct; my reputation was made by sticking up for myself. It was the law that counted on the roof, in the ally, on the street, or in the west side. Mom ruled.

Chapter Three

The Chair

As I mentioned before, my dad worked for a foreign pharmaceutical company and was often gone from home three weeks out of a month, several times a year. We lived out on Burr Street now, and there were more of us, too. With my mother in charge, my brothers and I would play, either in the front yard or across the street in the schoolyard. We preferred the schoolyard because the front yard was too close to my mom for comfort. All she had to do was walk out on the front porch, and she could decide who was eligible for some work detail. So, it was the schoolyard for us. There was actually a stretch of wood that ran the length of the block on the other side of the street from our house, and it was about one hundred and fifty yards deep before you got to the schoolyard. This buffer was a blessing because you could find a blind spot through which my mom could not see us, and, when she yelled, we would drop to the ground, and we were safe from her gaze. Later, we would claim that we didn't hear her from all the noise. Yes, we were over there, but we were not in the usual spot; we'd explain that some big kids were chasing us out, so we were further over. It worked every time.

When my dad was home, quite often on Saturday night, he would take my mom to the parish hall for a Knights of Columbus dance. They would tell us to behave, inform us of the times that various boys had to go to bed, what we could eat, and, if there was a problem, "to turn on the front porch light." We would all be on our best behavior. These nights were something special, very special. It was football under the lights, Saturday night football under the lights.

Our living room was big, at least for that day. I would estimate it was about twenty to twenty-five feet long. It seemed huge after we removed all the furniture because, with a rather plush wool carpet, it was the perfect playing field. It was so much better than playing in the filthy garage which had so many potential injury-causing objects laying and hanging about. In the carpeted living room, it was as if we had artificial turf back in the '50s. Everyone had an item or two that they were responsible for, and the depository was the garage since Dad usually drove the short distance to the hall, but the woods separating the parish and school grounds from our side of the street was a mine field of holes everybody dug to discourage anyone from going through the woods after dark. No adult walked through those woods at night for fear of ankle and knee sprains. I don't know why we were so adamant about not wanting anyone going through the woods after dark, but I think it was related to the fact that we kept our drapes perpetually closed in our bedrooms. I'm sure that was it.

There were only two pieces we could not remove from the playing field: the big hutch with all the "special bone china dishes" and the huge kidney-shaped desk with all the important papers in it at the other end of the room. Each was wood; I mean hard wood like cherry and weighed a ton. They were the end zones. All you had to do was reach out and touch the ball to the wood, and you scored.

Some of the Schlosser boys with their folks about in 1957:
I'm at the top on the left, and along the bottom are (from left
to right) Greg, Dick, and Gary.

The older and bigger guys had a distinct advantage with our
reach, but my younger brothers never complained. We elders
would not have listened anyway. My grandma on my mom's side
knitted a football with brown yarn and stuffed it with rags, and
it was about half the size of a real football. It was easier to catch,
and, when you fell on it, it gave with you, and you didn't get the
wind knocked out of you. It was great. I think Grandma Coffey
understood a lot more than she let on. She knew we were up to
something way before all hell broke loose, and we'd got in
trouble.

My brothers and I liked Grandma Coffey, and we saw a lot of
her since she lived with us for part of the year after Grandpa
Coffey died. I never quite understood it, but my cousin, Doyle,
from Detroit was scared to death of my grandma, his aunt. "She
was mean, and Aunt Emma scared the hell out of me," he told me
later. On the other hand, his mom, Aunt Mildred, was a great
aunt to all of us, and her husband, Uncle Ted Manning, was wonderful. I always felt badly because Doyle dreaded my grandma,
and all of us loved my aunt and uncle. But none of us liked their

dog, Bounce. He was a Boston bull, and he'd nip at our heels and legs when we visited Detroit. We would sit on the stairs at the end of their living room and wait for him to go out on the glasses in the front porch that ran the length of the house. Then, we would break for the kitchen. Bounce wasn't allowed in the kitchen, I guess, because he never went in there. I always felt that kind of evened things out between his side of the family and mine. He had a mean-assed dog, and our grandma seemed to be mean to him. But, when I'd tell Doyle my reasoning, he'd just cock his head and look at me. He didn't even have to say it, and I knew what he was getting at: how can our dog balance out your grandma, Aunt Emma? He was ten years older than me and smart, so I was sure he had a point, but things still balanced out in my book.

This peculiar way of thinking brings me back to the ball game and "the chair." We would strip the living room except for the hutch and the desk. Everyone took something out to the garage. We'd set the lamps on the hutch and desk and turn them up all the way, then we'd pull the big thick drapes closed, we'd choose sides, and it was Notre Dame football in the suburbs of Grand Rapids.

This one particular night, all was going well, and my side drove down and scored. We kicked off as the other Notre Dame squad drove down and, eventually, scored against the desk end zone. It was bad enough that they scored, but something was terribly wrong. There was a breaking sound that came from the desk. What? Then, we all stopped, took a gulp, and imagined the impossible. Someone had forgotten to bring "the chair" out in the garage. The point was not who or even why; it was the inevitable consequence that this oversight and maiming would result in: "She'll murder us in our sleep."

The desk was my dad's. I think he worked in one of the famous Grand Rapids furniture companies right after high school, while he was attending college. I can't imagine him having swiping it; it was too damned heavy. On the other hand, I can't imagine him buying it; it had to be really expensive. Well, at any rate, it was his, but the chair, which accompanied it, was my mom's. It sat with the legs and seat tucked under the desk and the back sticking up over the top of the desk. It wasn't just any chair; it was *the* chair. It was from Ireland. The families, the Quainns, the Doyles, the Mannings, the Kellys, and the Coffeys, had passed it on to my mother because she was the oldest in her generation. She was the "matriarch" in waiting. She knew all the families, all the great-great-grandparents, great-uncles and great-aunts, regular uncles and aunts, grandparents, cousins, second cousins, and cousins once and twice removed. She not only knew the genealogy, but she knew most of the people in the genealogy. She was to be the matriarch of the clans in the United States of America.

The chair was maybe made of rosewood, and the seat was fabric with a needlepoint design. It was like the throne or something. Sometimes, she would yell at us to come to supper and to get off the throne. That throne was the toilet. She said that throne was called the throne because the English thought they were so hoity-toity, and their monarch sat on this kind of throne. Needless to say, we never referred to "the chair" as a, or the, throne. It was quite simply known as "the chair." It was Mom's. It was from Ireland. It was more important than her relic of Saint Francis—he was Italian, not Irish. Mom said he was a good egg all the same, but he wasn't Irish. "'Tis a shame," she used to say.

Someone had failed to remove "the chair." It had remained parked at the desk, the seat and legs protected under the desk. But the back, sticking up and vulnerable, was now broken off. "The chair's" back was a continuation of the back legs. It ran up probably eighteen inches or so above the seat. At the top was a crosspiece that had an ornate carving in the center, and halfway down to the seat was another crosspiece, making it look a little like a small ladder. But it wasn't a ladder. It was "the chair"—Mom's "chair"—from the family and from Ireland.

"Jesus, Mary, and Joseph," someone said.

"Oh God," said another. The prayers were too late.

The next utterance was simply, "Shit."

The one that followed was more to the point: "She is going to kill us."

The next one was coldly descriptive: "She'll murder us in our sleep."

Damn, these comments were frightening and a distinct possibility. When it came to Ireland, her family, Notre Dame, and the Catholic Church, she was serious, dead serious. There were just some things in life that one did not screw around with, and the Old Sod, family, Notre Dame, and the Church were untouchable. We had violated two of the four most important things in her life. You didn't have to be a math major to know that was half of them, fifty percent of them. "Shit." We were dead. "Damn." We were seriously dead. She'd do it in our sleep; that was some satisfaction. Wait, no, it wasn't. We'd all lie there all night not sleeping, but waiting for her to murder us. We would see it coming. "Shit. Shit. Shit, and more shit."

She will start with the oldest since they are more at fault than the younger ones. The only satisfaction would be that we older ones would not witness the murder of our younger brothers. We hadn't known them as long, but, for the most part, we elders felt they were all right. Would she just choose any of the older ones at random or would she systematically go by age? Maybe by birthdays? Maybe size? "Aw shit, what difference would it make? We're all dead."

The back was broken completely off at the seat. There was no chance of fixing it. None of us went to public schools, so we didn't have wood shop or any classes that might have come in handy now. We knew we couldn't screw it. No neighbor could help us; they were all at the dance with my folks. Taping it was out of the question. We had no wood glue in the house that any of us knew about.

Someone said, "We're dead."

So, while the rest of the boys were bringing the furniture back in from the garage in silence and with a strained sense of purpose, the older brothers held a powwow. For some reason, God only knows why, it was suggested and decided to just get rid of "the chair." "Yeah, just get rid of it." We never considered for a moment the idea of just waiting up and telling Mom when she came home—no, no, no. That was out of the question. Not one of us suggested that, and I suspect some of us never even thought of that option. Telling her was not an option. Watching the hurt, the pain, and the agony that she would go through hearing us try to explain the disaster and then to see the mutilation, the castration, the sacrilege we had committed to the "sacred chair" would be too much for us to bear. Then, to witness the anger, the rage, and the tempest that was about to descend upon us was too much. We'd simply have to dispose of the evidence. We would get rid of "the chair."

As I think back on it now, and, indeed, every time I have thought of that decision since that fateful night, I cannot, for the life of me, figure out why that made sense, really. In hindsight, it makes no sense, none at all. As a matter of fact, it was stupid with a capital "S." Maybe it was the passion of the moment. We were scared to death. We just decided to get rid of "the (now broken) chair."

My grandma was living in Detroit with Aunt Mildred and Uncle Ted (and scaring my cousin, Doyle), but her old Pontiac was parked on the side of the driveway. We elders found the keys, went out, and started it up. We carefully carried the mutilated carcass of "the chair" out to the car, and, with considerable respect, laid it in the trunk. The three of us decided who would drive. None of us had our driver's licenses, but we were on a mission now, and we were not deterred by such menial things as licenses. We all sat in the front seat and drove as one. We wanted to put even now as much distance between us and the victim as possible. I, for one, thought anyone in the backseat on this ride might find themselves attacked by the not yet dead victim, thrusting through the back of the rear seat to avenge our dastardly deed like you'd see in some monster movie. We negotiated the turn at the end of the driveway and the one at the end of our street. We slowly made our way past our neighbor's houses up to the rectory on the corner of the main street. We stopped and took another right onto Clyde Park Avenue. We all looked into Resurrection Cemetery. Grandma's car was like a hearse and we were going to a funeral for "the chair." But the thought was never far from us that "we were dead." We traveled about two or three mile until we came to a swamp along the side of the road. We pulled over and turned the lights out so as not to attract any attention. We unlatched the trunk, respectfully withdrew the dismembered "chair," and two of us hurled the two pieces as far as we could into the swamp.

There was no prayer service, eulogy, or commemoration of any kind. We simply disposed of the evidence. There was a collective sigh of relief, and we headed home. Backing the Pontiac into the exact place was tricky, but we managed it. Entering the house, we found everything in its place—well, almost everything. We checked on the little ones. They were so innocent. They were all fast asleep.

"What the hell, they're as guilty as we are. We won't be getting any sleep tonight," I said. "They're young and stupid. We're all gonna die."

We double-checked everything in the living room. Then, we remembered the snacks the folks had left for us in the kitchen. They were still there and had to be eaten; otherwise, they'd know something was wrong. In silence, we polished off what we knew was our "last supper," and we headed off to bed. We left one lamp on at the far end of the living room at the opposite end from the desk.

There was a chance they wouldn't notice the gaping cavity under the desk. "Yeah, a snowball's chance in hell." There was no hope for us. Hope anticipated that there was a snowball's chance. There was really no hope. So, we wished for it. Wishing suggests there is no hope; you just "wish" it would. Or, in our case, that it wouldn't happen. But, really, there was not a snowball's chance in hell of that happening or not happening. I actually said goodbye to my brothers instead of good night. "We were as good as dead."

It wasn't long before they returned. I heard them in the kitchen taking care of the dishes we'd left out. Then, there was a pause. We all held our breath and expected the door to our bedroom to burst open and for her to enter in a warp spasm like some possessed banshee looking for the guilty. All hell was about to break loose.

I wondered if I should fight back. That would be natural, I suppose. But it was my mom. I was guilty after all. I deserved what was in store for me, but I'd fight back all the same. I think she would respect that. There was sound coming from the bathroom now and, in a matter of minutes, all the lights were off, and there was silence. She'd come like a banshee in the darkness of night. But, nothing as minutes passed. We all exhaled, but sleep did not come that night. In our room, we all just laid on our backs and looked at the ceiling. After hours had passed, it was getting light outside, and we stirred because some of us had to serve early Sunday mass because most of us were altar boys.

Living across the street and through the "church woods" from the church, my brothers and I usually got the early masses to serve. Mom was surprised we were up without having to be called. We gave her some flimsy excuse, which she paid no mind to because she was still tired from dancing, I suppose. Off we went doing everything very devoutly because we were sure she would have noticed by the time we got home, and infanticide would be the rule, but nothing. Other brothers came and went to serve mass all morning, and nothing was seen, neither was anything done. Of course, we all avoided the living room, which was difficult because the television was in that room, and we all liked watching TV.

The whole day went off without so much as a word about "the chair." Surely, it would happen on Sunday night. So, another sleepless night followed, with most of us staring at the ceiling the whole night except for some moments of sleep. When we would drift off for a few seconds, we would wake with a start. We'd breathe heavily for a minute, then calm down and try not to dose again.

On Monday, we rose at her call (there was no way we could be up before being called two days in a row without drawing Mom's attention to the odd occurrence). Off we went to school. This Monday was the shortest school day in our lives. This was true for those who went downtown to Catholic Central High School and those who went across the street to Saint John's Grade School. It seemed to no more than get started and it was over, and we had to start for home. It was a ragged homecoming because of the differences in distance, and that some of us played sports and had practice right after school. I was one of the last ones to get home; it was about six-thirty in the evening.

As I approached the house, everything seemed in order. But looks are deceiving. I carefully came around the back of the house and peered in the window of the so-called breakfast nook where we ate. All was normal. The gang was all there, and Mom was just starting to dish up food for the young ones. In I went, as innocent as the day.

None of us could stay awake on Monday night. We were all exhausted from the lack of sleep from the night before, and so, on Monday night, we slept like innocent babes. Tuesday morning came and went without a hitch. But our luck could not last, and I had a bad premonition all day. That night was a repeat of Monday night: I cautiously checked things out before I entered and took my seat for supper.

Now, my dad was home this week, so he officiated at saying the grace before our meal—so far, so good. Food was dished up for the wee ones, and, as the serving dishes with potatoes, beans, and meat made the circuit, my mother asked the long-awaited question, "Where's 'the chair?'" None of us batted an eye; neither did any of us pay any attention to her question. Then, she said in a louder voice, "I said where is 'the chair?'"

I should explain that in the breakfast nook, my mom sat at one end of the table nearest the actual kitchen, while my dad sat at the other end of the table nearest the phone. The boys were arranged along the sides with four of the older and bigger along one side and five of the smaller on the other side. Mom was one away from me on my right. The second time she asked the question got every one's attention. Everything stopped in mid-motion, and our gaze was drawn toward Mom. The silence was deafening. The air of doom hung over the table.

Shit, I thought. *We're not even going to get to taste it, let alone enjoy our last meal.*

It was obvious she was not going to repeat the question. The next sound would be an explanation, an admission, a confession. Indeed, a last confession. None of us had had an opportunity to go to confession with a priest; so, not only would we be executed without so much as tasting our last meal, but we would all "go to hell in a hand basket," as Mom liked to say in such situations. Just when it seemed that our end was at hand, my youngest and littlest brother, God love him, said the most brilliant thing in his short life, or his whole life for that matter. He sat next to Dad on the other side of the table from me, and he said in his squeaky little voice, "The last one I saw use it was Dad."

My mother's gaze parted the table as it bore down like twin lasers on my dad. We all turned toward my father in relief as he took the weight of ten pairs of accusing eyes. You cannot imagine the feeling of deliverance we collectively felt, I mean, actually felt in a physical way. Both sides of the table glared at my dad as only condemned men could who had been saved at the last minute. We tended to side with my mom because she was our mom, and, if the truth were known, in spite of the regular near-death experiences she subjected us to, we liked Mom best.

Dad could only muster, "What are you talking about? I didn't do anything to the 'chair.' I don't even remember sitting at the desk this past week."

I should reiterate that my little brother didn't exactly say Dad had done something to "the chair." He was simply saying that Dad was the last to be seen using it. He didn't even say it was this past week. But that was enough. The damage was done. My little brother didn't lie; he only stated a fact. None of us could sit in "the chair," and we had no business at, or in, the desk, so we were not suspected of having used the desk or "the chair." We weren't suspected of anything now. Mom had added one and one, and it was too bad for Dad. He used the desk to write out checks to pay bills, and he sat on "the chair" to do it. He didn't deny being the last and only one to have recently used "the chair." His defense was that he didn't remember—a likely excuse. He was guilty in Mom's eyes, and now, ours as well. My wee brother was a genius.

My mother always said that my dad and his family didn't like her side of the family. I've heard stories of why over the years, but, in essence, it came down to the clannish Irish, their drinking and smoking and carrying on I remember at wakes, the luncheons after the funeral at the parish hall, especially the get-togethers after all of the formal stuff that would convene at our house. My Irish relatives, from both Canada and across the United States, would stand around and tell the real stories that were not for all to hear. For us boys, it was a manhood ritual. The elders would gather in the kitchen and breakfast nook. They were mostly men who would stand while the few women would sit. They all smoked a lot. The kitchen and nook were like the top of a mountain touching the clouds.

The aunts would eventually move on to the living room to comfort whoever, and the older men would resume telling the private stories, some of which were secret even to their wives. They let us boys remain.

"It's good that you hear this," one of the ancients said. "But mum's the word." So, we stayed. I do not know which uncle said this because the smoke was so thick that you could not distinguish anyone of them from another. All we ever saw at such times were their legs, which all looked the same in their going to church Sunday suits (which were also worn on special occasions like wakes and funerals). We saw them so infrequently that we didn't recognize who was speaking. A voice simply came out of the clouds, like on Sinai. When I was little, all I ever saw were the legs of the elders because from the waste up, they were in the clouds of smoke.

I was too little to understand and get the stories back then. I just hung around in the kitchen area. Then, every couple of minutes, a voice would come out of the mist and say, "Roger (or Ruairi), me boy, another beer." A hand would come out of the cloud with a partially empty beer bottle for me to return to the garage.

There was always a swallow or two of beer left in the bottle. I was on my way to becoming one of them.

When I returned with an opened full bottle, the voice would say, "Ah, good boy, good boy. Did you get a taste?"

I would always answer, "Aye, thank you." I never saw the grin of approval, but I felt it. I really felt it. And it felt good.

These elders were mostly known from their belts down to their shoes, the smoke covering their torsos and heads. It was only at their funerals that I really ever looked them in the face as they lay there in the casket. Those thin, dark-complected, hardworking Irish men knew the stories, and slowly but surely, initiated my generation into knowledge and understanding of the stories and the people of Ireland and the Irish—my mother's people.

My dad and his people didn't like the clannishness, the drinking until it was all gone, the smoking, the telling of the stories, and the whispering of the real stories that were meant for only "us" to hear.

I remember Grandma Coffey holding me in her arms once when I was still rather small and young. Grandma Schlosser came over to talk to us (to me actually).

Grandma Coffey asked me, "Which grandma do you like best?"

Although I was quite young, I knew I would hurt one or the other of them, so I just said, "I don't know, both."

That's how the Irish were; they would lay it on the line, with no compromise, and it was all or nothing. My dad's people really despised that. Germans were supposedly calculating, reserved, and more polite than to ask such questions and put a small tyke like me in such a spot. Grandma Coffey was Irish, and so was her daughter, my mother, and her sons were on their way to becoming true Irish Americans. Away from Ireland, you aren't simply born Irish; you become Irish. You grow into it. It's a process that results in the product. Just because your mom and/or your dad are Irish, that does not ensure that you are Irish. Parents alone do not make you Irish. You become Irish by being initiated into the family, the clans, the stories, the hushed secrets, and, over time, by understanding the totality of it all. We Schlosser boys were becoming Irish more and more. At the wakes, one end of the spectrum was dropping off, but, at the other end, a new generation was embracing and becoming Irish.

It was as if Mom was a gardener who was cultivating a new generation of Irish fruits or vegetables. She cared for us; she watered, weeded, and fertilized the ground under and around us. She made sure that neither weeds nor birds nor rabbits nor other varmints harmed us. We were her prized produce and nothing was going to harm or prevent this harvest from being a prize-winning assortment. She often used the analogy that she was "a petunia in an onion patch."

Dad and his family were not thrilled with these developments. We older boys celebrated Saint Patrick's Day with an enthusiasm that only real Irishmen know. We celebrated Notre Dame victories as only Irish Catholic Americans can. Later, we also cheered for Boston College as only Irish Catholic Americans can, except when they played the Irish from South Bend. It all had an edge to it, and Dad didn't like it.

So, Mom's conclusion that Dad used the chair last and did away with it was feasible. Hell, it was brilliant. It was Irish, an Irish conclusion drawn from centuries of history. She gritted her teeth, those carnivorous teeth that I had nearly tempted way back on the west side of Grand Rapids so long ago. I could see her mind working through the small slits between her teeth. I could imagine her thinking: "weren't the Anglo-Saxon forefathers of the English Germans?" Yah, or "*Ja*" to be exact. That was it, enough said.

Indeed, Mom never said another thing in front of us boys about "the chair." A poor substitute was found to replace the real thing, "the chair." I suspect that my dad's life was a little more difficult with regard to his relationship with Mom from then on. As far as I know, a lot changed in the privacy of their bedroom because of her suspicions about "the chair." She never got pregnant again, that much I know for sure. Years passed, and it was never mentioned, but my mom's relatives seemed even more reserved, no, distant toward my dad than before. The Coffeys, Quainns, Doyles, Mannings, and Kellys were never reserved. But, I think the whole episode was discussed with the clans. In her solitude concerning "the chair," my mom resigned herself to holding my dad responsible, and, when it was in her power, she also held him accountable. The truth of the matter was Mom never seemed to be truly happy unless she was "pissed," sorry, "got her Irish up," over something. She was plenty "pissed" over "the chair." She "got her Irish up" for years after that fateful discovery. A pale settled over my dad, and he was never quite the same either.

As the years and some of my brothers passed, the whole ugly episode was never mentioned. My mother's silence concerning "the chair" and the discovery of the guilty party was never mentioned for twenty-five years or more. But the tormented expressions of Dad periodically punctuated the conspiracy of silence, but none ever felt a pang of guilt. Dad had set himself up for the fall, and Mom became a victim of her own character, past and present. I was content to let sleeping dogs lie.

Now, I should explain, many of my brothers were not too tightly wrapped, which is polite for saying they were out to lunch, if not really slow, or even bordering on stupidity. You get the point. To illustrate this point, let me digress for a few paragraphs. Uncle Ted Coffey, my mom's brother, lived around the corner on Floyd Street about six doors down from Burr Avenue. He and his wife had almost as many kids as we had, but some of them were girls. We'd go to their house for Thanksgiving, and they'd come to our house for Christmas. The next year, we'd switched off, and they'd come to our house for Thanksgiving, and we'd go to theirs for Christmas. Regardless, something was going to get busted in the basement before we ate or after we ate. We always played football, us against them.

My uncle's basement had a furnace with ducts called "the octopus" because it had all these big ducts going out of it in upward angles. We must have knocked about three or four of them down and trampled them to pieces before "all hell broke loose." We left before desert, which was a shame because Aunt Rosemary made the best cheesecake in the whole world. We were marched home to be beaten. My mom's arm was so sore from hitting us that she announced a new policy: picture this if you can, four of us would be beaten before we went to Uncle Ted's from now on, and the rest would get it when we got home. Everyone knew we were going to break something and get a beating, so she figured she'd spread out the beatings and save her arm from fatigue. The problem for her was that she couldn't remember which of us got it going and who was to get it returning from the outing.

When we would return home, she'd grab us one by one as we came through the backdoor, and she'd ask us if we had been spanked yet. Several of my brothers would admit that, "No, I didn't get it yet." So, she would beat them. How dumb was that on their part? I figured out from the start that you should answer, "Yeah, I got it before, and it still hurts." She couldn't remember, so she'd say, "Okay," and in I would go. As I said, some of my brothers were short a few watts. What was that old saying? "The lights were on, but no one was home." Can you imagine any one admitting "no?"

Again, I mentioned this incident to illustrate the questionable judgments and problem-solving abilities of some of my brothers. Now, we can return to the long-forgotten issue of "the chair." After twenty-five years or so, the bubble burst. We were all out at the folk's cottage, celebrating their wedding anniversary I think. My brother, Greg, was feeling no pain when he sat in an aluminum folding lawn chair. Some of the nylon strips started to rip, and, as he tried to get out of the chair on the lawn by the lake, the chair actually folded up a bit with him in it. He was rolling around on the ground yelling, "The chair's biting my ass." It was truly funny. The chair was twisted up, bent, and rendered useless. But then, he did something that still baffles me, and if the truth was known, "pissed" me off to this day. He blurted out, "Do you remember 'the chair?' How we broke it and you older guys got rid of it?" The silence that descended on the lake was total. Birds stopped chirping. Frogs stopped croaking. Boats stopped running. Mothers gathered up their children and got them inside their cottages.

There were only four of us boys alive by that time, and I figured that number was in serious jeopardy because of Greg's injudicious timing and rash admission. He was flirting with death, and being accessories, we were marked for death as well. She was a lot older, but she still had the capacity for mass murder. Knowing all of the variables, I scanned the yard for my wife and kids, and I just pointed toward the car and started heading that way myself, keeping an eye on Mom the whole time. Greg was still rolling around on the ground with his chair biting his ass; Dick and Gary were still too stunned to react at this point. They were still immobile, and looking at Mom, then Greg, then Dad, then back to Mom, Greg, and Dad. They were not exactly frozen in a time warp, but they had certainly short-circuited. As for me, I was moving for the car.

Today, I find that part of the story still funny. But I'm still pissed at my brother who's been dead for several years now. He damn well nearly got us killed a second time over "the chair." As

I think back now, I think "the chair" was his responsibility to be taken care of that fateful night so long ago. To this day, I can only imagine what was going through Mom's mind, and, for that matter, Dad's that day. I never asked, and no one ever said specifically. The rest of the day was anticlimactic, to say the least.

In the intermittent years those of us boys still alive had gone our separate ways, gotten married, had children, and put the great sacrilege to rest. We all lived good lives in the Grand Rapids area. All of that was threatened because of Greg's poor judgment. Mom never moved from the front of the cottage. I thought, for sure, Greg was a goner. Mom could hold some of the grandkids for hostage until we returned and turned ourselves over to her devices. But it didn't happen. I wondered what was up. She hadn't gotten soft in her old age, if anything her "Irish" thing had deepened and intensified. But what was it? As I got myself and mine alongside of the cottage, I realized the danger was non-existent. Mom was not herself. I studied Mom for some time, catching Greg still rolling around out of the corner of my eye. It was an absurd contradiction.

But it took me a moment longer to get the bigger picture. She wasn't looking at Greg or me or any of the others. What was she fixed on?

Then, I saw. It was my dad. He was just standing there, up near the porch, tending the grill. The expression on his face was like he had seen a miracle, a ghost, or maybe a colossal train wreck. His mouth was open, his shoulders sagged, and the grill spatula hung in his hand at his side. He was in disbelief. He couldn't quite process what he had just heard. But then, he began to fathom it. After all these years, he just heard the truth, the truth that his sons had conspired against him. His wife, my mother, had held him accountable all these years. The harm, the accusations, the incredibility of it all was overwhelming. Poor Dad, he looked pathetic. I wouldn't have noticed any of this at all if Mom had "gotten her Irish up." But she hadn't. We all just stood there, gazing back and forth between Mom and Dad. Then, Mom broke the ice.

She said, "Well, I guess you didn't do it. But, I know you would have liked to, and that's just as bad. You deserved what you got."

My dad's slow-to-form anger was immediately replaced by self-pity. He just turned back to the grill and slowly exhaled. My mom started to laugh and so did all of us. It wasn't a nervous laugh; it was a laugh that comes to those who have pulled off a good one, and now, it is exposed for all to see and know. Oh, the relief was there, and it was genuine. For some, it was finally getting it all off their chest. But, for me, it was that we were to live another day because Katie O'Coffey was still perfectly capable of mass murder. After all these years, she had discovered the facts and was still satisfied with her original assessment. Did I mention that Mom was Irish?

A picture of my mom from about the time of "the chair" incident, enjoying Holland State Park on Lake Michigan

Chapter Four

Vacations

At our house, vacations were always a mixed bag. My folks, well, my dad, could not possibly please everyone, so there were always mixed feelings, hurt feelings, bruised feelings, before we ever set off. We were going where he decided. He loved several places, but "out west," the "Smokies," and the American "old west" were his favorites. "Out west" constituted the Dakotas, the State of Wyoming, especially Jackson Hole, the Grand Tetons, Yellowstone National Park, and, eventually, Glacier National Park. He also loved the Smoky Mountains, centered on Gatlinburg, Tennessee. After I was out of the house, he turned to the "South West." That was Arizona, Nevada, New Mexico, Utah, and Southern California. Now, it was difficult to argue with someone about the value of visiting such places, but there were other spots that ranked high on Mom's list and our (the boys') places to visit. But Dad's choices were the choices time after time, year in and year out, vacation after vacation. One of my brothers casually mentioned that these places didn't seem to change year after year, except for the growing traffic and crowds. It took us longer and longer to queue up and see the attractions again this year. We would pray for rain just to break the monotony.

Dad got a full month of vacation each year, so we could cover distances for weeks at a time unless Mom's toleration and nerves wore thin. There were no family vans back in the '50s and early '60s, so a station wagon it was. Try to imagine the whole gang heading off to Yellowstone National Park in a station wagon. It doesn't take much to imagine the seating arrangement on these excursions—Dad and Mom in the front seat, with one of us sitting between them and one on Mom's lap. Obviously, this was a time way before child safety seat laws had been considered. There would be four of us jammed into the middle seat with the rest in the rear. We had a Chevy station wagon on several trips and the rear seat faced out the rear. One of my brothers, I think it was Dick, got terribly car sick, so if he got stuck in the back, he would crawl into the cramped space between the rear and middle seat. He was like a wiener in a bun. He'd throw the stuff that was packed in that spot down into his seat and would fall fast asleep. If he didn't get to sleep quickly he would get nauseated and puke. That was always exciting and fun to deal with, especially if he wouldn't make it out of the car. My mom would go "stark raving mad" as she used to say. We'd be in a parking lot, or along the side of a road, and my mom would be cleaning up barf from the inside of the car. My dad couldn't look at vomit without getting the heaves himself.

Some of my fondest memories were being awakened in the middle of the night because my dad would have stepped in our dog's vomit. Our dog, Gypsy, was about ten years old when she developed a sensitive stomach. She inevitably would eat something that she should not have had. My brothers fed her everything and anything. It wasn't that they were being mean to Gypsy; they just knew she would get sick, and, if my dad were home, he would take her outside. But old Gypsy never got outside. She was breaking down rapidly and was fading fast. She'd start to run for the front door (Yeah, the damn dog got to use the front door, but my brothers and I couldn't until we were married. Go figure. It's an Irish thing I guess), but as soon as she was off the living room carpet and on the vestibule tile floor, she'd throw up. Dad would step on it, and the fun would begin.

He'd start to get the dry heaves. He'd be gagging, making himself nearly throw up, with his stomach contracting, and he'd get the dog out the front door. He'd be calling for my mother to help him get the dog barf off his foot, out from between his toes, and the smell would set off a new round of his heaves.

My mom would be ridiculing him, "For God's sake, be quiet."

About this time, we would all be awake and just rolling in our beds in laughter. If he stopped gagging before we thought it was time, one of my brothers would mimic the sound of Dad's heaving, and Dad would immediately and automatically start all over again.

Mom would start in on Dad again, and when she heard us choking back the laughter, she'd yell, "Knock it off you guys or I'll come in there and knock you into the middle of next week."

It was all great fun and worth being awakened for an hour or so on these nights.

When we were older, I remember one of us retorted that being "knocked into the middle of next week" wouldn't be so bad; we'd miss a lot of school. The giggling and muffled laughing would start again until Mom threatened real violence. At two or three in the morning, she was in no mood to be tempted. She was always perfectly capable of mass murder. But hearing Dad get those heaves was like music to our ears. We would wake up from a dead sleep. No one woke us up. We'd hear him at the other end of the house, and it was like a fire alarm for laughter. We would lay there in our beds, convulsing in laughter.

One other trick we learned at an early age had to do with the old sugar cubes one would get in restaurants for coffee. Whenever we went to a restaurant, which we did occasionally on Sunday afternoons or evenings, we older boys would load up on sugar cubes. Each of us would have five or six of the cubes in our pockets for use later when we got home. When we got home, we would unwrap them, pop five or six in our mouths, and extend our arms from our sides and spin around like a top. We got terribly dizzy, and the sugar would turn us green with a hint of yellow, and we'd get the heaves. If we made it into the house and blew lunch there, it would set my dad off as well as my mom. He'd get the heaves, she'd be yelling at him, and the verdict of food poisoning at the restaurant kept us home from school on a lot of Mondays.

My brother, Dick, would get that way by simply staying awake in the car for more than ten minutes. Sometimes, we would purposely prevent him from getting to the space between the seats. He'd whine to my folks, and Mom would threaten to have my dad pull the station wagon over to the side of the road, and she'd "end the problem then and there." But by this time, Dick was overcome with motion sickness, and it was showtime. He never seemed to be able to exit the auto in time, so there was barf landing somewhere within the vehicle. We'd be sitting there while my dad was making the heaving noise, and my mom was cleaning up, aiming her disgust and sarcasm at my dad for being so squeamish. We would try not to laugh out loud so as not to deflect her ire from my dad. This was not necessarily an easy trick.

To return to the Yellowstone story, we just seemed to crawl along. It took most of the first day just to get to Chicago. These were the days before freeways. We were told that "if we were good," we'd "see Chicago." We were going to see the city whether we were good or not. You had to go past it on the way to Davenport, Iowa and the "Mighty Mississippi River." We humored the folks and settled in for a long trip. Chicago was all right, but then, we were bribed with the Mississippi: "We'll cross it if you are good." The older of us knew we were going to cross it to head west whether we were good or not. We humored the folks and kept our mouths shut and shook our heads for the younger ones to see. We'd show the little ones a map later on and explain the geography to them. "To get there, we have to cross here, period. 'Good' my ass. It was simple logistics. We let the folks think they were fooling us with that 'good' crap. We knew what was going on." If it was a revelation to the young ones, it was affirmation to us elders that we could bring this whole thing to a screeching halt anytime we wished.

The first day was always the most difficult because we inevitably got a late start; then Dick would get sick, and there was always the traffic around Chicago. We stayed some place in Iowa. My dad would go out early in the morning and find a gallon of milk, and we would eat some cereal for breakfast, and then, we were on the road early. Lunches were based around sliced bologna, a loaf of bread, lettuce, mustard, and ketchup. If we had been good, we also got potato chips. Evening meals were long, drawn-out affairs since there were no fast food places like McDonald's or Burger King.

On one trip, a serious riot broke out in the middle seat, about two hours into the second day. Mom was hampered from hitting us because she was holding one of the little ones on her lap. She would be yelling and swinging over her head and wildly over the back of her seat. She just couldn't make contact. She finally told my dad to pullover. The road was narrow with little shoulder room. Corn, eight feet high, came nearly out to the road. It was like a canyon, a "corn canyon."

Dad came around to the passenger side and had the four of us get out from the middle seat. We were all pretty nervous that Mom would get out and kill us by the side of the road. Should we try and run up the road? A truck would probably hit us because there were a large number of huge trucks whizzing by on this two-lane road. Even to us, that road was not safe. Maybe safety was to be found in the rows of nearby corn. But we could surely get lost out there. I, for one, was not sure that being lost in a cornfield in Iowa was the way to go. Let me correct myself. It would not be being lost in an Iowa cornfield; rather, I would be lost in the cornfield called Iowa. I'd never seen so much corn in my life. But this observation would have to wait. There were more pressing issues at hand.

Mom didn't get out of the auto, but she rolled her window down, and she shouted instructions to my dad. He was getting sick of her badgering, so he placed himself between Mom and us. This was a precarious spot because it was a two-lane highway with minimum shoulder space. Iowa roads had a little lip on the shoulder of the road, and it was easy to catch a right tire on it if the gravel had worn away. Huge trucks were whizzing by and making a racket, swaying the station wagon and throwing up dust and stones. Dad's back was to her, and we were facing the vehicle, Mom, and the road.

He looked tired. His only question for the moment was, "What's going on?"

Greg said, "Rog hit me."

Dad looked at me and said, "Why did you hit your brother?"

Well, there were a thousand reasons why someone hits their brother, but the most immediate and convincing was, "He stinks."

Dad dropped his shoulders and exhaled in a gesture of exhaustion and a total lack of understanding. "Greg always stinks," was his feeble reply. In the meantime, Mom was getting her two cents in, and it was looking as if she might still intervene.

But then, Dad said to Gary, "Why did you hit Rog?"

Gary explained, "When he reared back to tag Greg he bumped me so I let him have it."

Dad said to the next brother, Dick, who, as usual, was sick, "And you?"

"Gary bumped me," Dick explained, "and I feel sick."

Now, Mom seemed to be getting more agitated every minute.

Dad finely turned and said to her, "Calm yourself. You aren't helping the situation any."

"*Well*, I thought, *let's hear it for dad. Dad was naïve, but he was also reasonable*. And then, my hopes died.

Dad simply asked, "Give me one good reason why I shouldn't just leave you here. Maybe that's what I'll do. I'll just leave you four here. You guys be here in two weeks from today. Be on the other side of the road, and, in two weeks time, we will be coming through on the way home, and we'll pick you up."

Damn! I couldn't think of a good reason not to be left. I was baffled. I would expect this sort of option from my mom, after she had beaten us for a while. But coming from Dad, well, this left me numb and dumb.

After an agonizing ten or fifteen seconds, my brother, Gary, I think, made sweeping outward gestures with his hands and arms and simply said, "Because it's Iowa."

Gee, that was brilliant. That was the precise answer that was both accurate and valid. Even my dad had to laugh. Mom wanted to know who said something and what was it he said.

Dad exhaled loudly again, turned to my mom, and said, "Nothing. It's all right," and he gave us all more of a smirk than a smile and said, "Get in and behave. The next stop, if you're acting better, is the Corn Palace in Mitchell, South Dakota."

Hell, that was a state away, and, if I were a betting man, I would say at least one or two mid-seat riots away as well. As I said, Dad was naïve as well as reasonable.

For all the grief we gave him, I never remember my dad spanking or beating us. He always acted hurt at our misbehavior; Mom, on the other hand, simply saw our misbehavior as an excuse to "get her Irish up." There are some people who aren't happy unless they are pissed at something, and Mom was one of those people. In hindsight, I guess my brothers and I must have intuitively seen our misbehavior as setting the stage for Mom to be happy; although, I must admit, this thought came to me later in life. The truth was very simple: we were just plain naughty. There were so many of us that what one was just thinking of doing, two others were probably already doing it. We must have driven her to the brink of going nuts nearly every day.

It was on this same trip that Gary had been complaining about a loose tooth for about four days, even before we left on the vacation, and for hundreds of miles. We pulled into a gas station, and we took turns going to the toilet. I happened to go with Gary, who continued to whine about his loose tooth.

Finally, I said, "Here I'll fix it." I belted him one in the mouth, and sure enough, I knocked his tooth out.

He was still crying when we got out to the station wagon. I had knocked out the wrong tooth. I heard about that for about two hundred miles. Deep down, I think Mom thought it was kind of funny, but she put on this act that she was upset. On we went, further into the west.

I whispered to Gary, "That tooth fairy isn't going to find you way out here. You're screwed."

That wound him up, and he was bawling and carrying on. I think I set a record with that one. We hadn't gone a mile, and only a minute elapsed since the last crises. Yeah, that had to be a record.

The Corn Palace was a bust. Ears of corn attached to a building, making a mosaic of design and pictures of one sort or another. Devils Tower was cool. Mom wanted to leave some of us there, saying, "We'd feel right at home with the devil." Rapid City, South Dakota, with the Dinosaur Park was awesome as were the Bad Lands. Cody, Wyoming was really "the west" all right. And then, there was Yellowstone National Park. The deer, buffalo, moose, and bears made the trip magical from this point on, and there were no fights at all now. This place was special. This was a world all its own. We were in awe of this place. We went down for a day to the Grand Tetons and Jackson Hole. We stayed about a week in the park, eating at outdoor cookouts, chuckwagon style buffets, at Old Faithful Lodge. What a week. I'm amazed that none of my brothers fell into the hot thermal springs and scalded himself to death or got mauled by bears or gored by a buffalo. Most of the time, we were wild, reckless, and went full throttle. In fact, all of us were trouble with a capital "T."

Dad also took great delight in telling the younger boys the story about a certain Yellowstone bear and showing my younger brothers the exact spot where the story unfolded. Since this particular story involved me and me alone, and I had relived it through my dad's telling of the story and nightmares I had for years after the actual event, I had no interest in hearing it again. This time, I exhaled and wandered off to await Old Faithful.

The nightmares became less frequent over about a forty-year span, but, even in middle age, I would wake up in the middle of the night and in a cold sweat after having "the dream about the bear." The psychologists and psychiatrists and MDs my dad consulted with said the nightmares would subside, and if I lived long enough, would eventually cease altogether. In fact, they did, eventually.

In the late '40s, there were just a few of us, and I was nearly five years old when Dad decided we were going to Yellowstone National Park. It was one of his favorite places. It was also a long trip that year, too. In Yellowstone, we stayed in a little log cabin that was one of about forty strung along a walking commons near the Old Faithful Lodge and geyser. There were about twenty cabins on each side of this pedestrian mall that ran between the cabins and the front, and only the door of each cabin faced the open walk area that headed to the lodge or the geyser. Autos were parked in the back or on the side of the cabins. I don't know if we hauled the bedding or if it was supplied, but my mom was busy setting up the beds, and my dad was unpacking the car.

Having been stuck in the car with even an abbreviated group at this point, you can imagine my desire to get away from them all.

"Don't go far. We are all going to see Old Faithful go off in about half an hour," Dad said as I wandered down the open area toward a group of people who were intrigued by something in the middle of the pedestrian mall about five cabins away.

It turned out to be a bear stuck in a trashcan. The cans, about the size of a fifty-five-gallon drum, but shorter, were sort of fenced in to prevent them from being tipped over, obviously by bears. This bear had nosedived into the can, and it didn't fall over so he was stuck. He was in a foul mood, and people were taking pictures of this bear's fanny sticking out of the can. It was sort of funny, until he flopped out.

Someone yelled, "Run."

Everyone took off, including me.

My problem was I couldn't find our cabin; they all looked exactly the same. I wasn't really running. I was loping while my eyes searched for something familiar, like our car or my folks or my brothers. All at once, something hit me and knocked me down and forward. I ended up under a car parked next to a cabin. Fortunately, back in the '40s, automobiles sat well off the ground, and there was room for me to roll right under the car. When I sort of came to, the first thing I noticed was that the bear was reaching for me under the car.

Someone was yelling, "He's after the kid. Get him," or something like that.

Some guys chased the bear off, and I came out of the other side of that car like a shot and spotted our car parked in back of a cabin on the other side of the mall, just one cabin down. I didn't open the screen door. I blew right threw it and wedged myself in a back corner, eyes wide open.

Mom stood up, but before she could yell at me, the crowd rushed up and said, "A bear had come out of a trashcan and chased the boy, swiping at him and hitting him, so he rolled under a parked car."

"No, no, he wasn't tormenting the bear. He was just watching when the bear got out of the can and started chasing him down the walkway. He ran in here. Is he yours? Is he okay?"

I was checked by a park ranger and, eventually, by a park doctor. Not a scratch, just some bruising. The doctor said, "He was lucky. He's bruised and will be a little sore. Give him baby aspirin; he'll be as good as new."

I felt all right, but I was nervous to be alone, and I didn't feel comfortable with fury critters anymore. Part of my rehab involved placing me in the presence of stuffed furry animals like teddy bears and, in due course, to have me play with kittens and puppies, the cats and dogs, followed by trips to zoos and museums. My dad wanted a family picture in front of a stuffed grizzly in the Old Faithful Lodge just a day after the attack. That wasn't going to happen with me in the picture.

We rode home with a big, stuffed teddy bear in the backseat. I threw it out the window twice as we were driving along on the way home. Dad thought he was using psychology in helping me recover from my traumatic moment. Actually, he was just pissing me off and adding to the storehouse of resentment that lifts its ugly head throughout these stories with regards to my dad. In case you haven't caught it yet, he does not fare well throughout this journal.

When we got home, the bear was left outside of my bedroom door each night. I was not pleased. Then, one morning, the damn bear was in my bedroom. I was not pleased, so I tried to light it on fire. I was actually getting away with a lot of bad behavior because my dad thought it was psychological reaction to the….well, you know. When we moved shortly thereafter out to the Village of Ars, we got a dog. I hated that damn dog. He didn't get the dog for any of the right reasons. Dad got the dog because he thought the dog was therapy. Dad was convinced he could psych out a five-year-old kid. He was only kidding himself.

Some therapy after my session with the bear at Yellowstone Park in 1949; as can be seen, I am not a happy camper.

For years and years after that fateful trip, every time friends and neighbors, relatives and acquaintances would ask, "Which one was attacked by the bear?" Dad would go through the whole story as if he saw it all, as if he participated in some aspect of the attack or rescue. This was the first time I noticed my dad enhancing a story, my story at that, with his chosen embellishments. He was trying to be an Irish storyteller. He was trying to out-Irish the Irish. Was it jealousy, or was it that he thought he could match or outmatch Mom's side of the family? These questions were bad enough, but, over the years, we boys observed that Dad would tell a version of a story which we all knew to be false. He wasn't doing it to be funny with us or to kid us; he just decided to keep repeating things over and over, so that he started to believe them. The rest of us all knew they were BS (ironically, his initials!). He eventually convinced himself that his version really happened. His version wasn't for aesthetic purpose or to be funny or anything like that. He just wanted to change reality. As he got older, especially after my mom died, he really got worse with distorting reality in negative ways. My last remaining brother and I found it more and more difficult to tolerate his mean and selfish stories. Maybe he was just getting back at us for all the stuff we subjected him to as related in these stories. If that is the case, I understand, but he still did it in bad taste.

The moral to the story: if you are going to practice poetic license with regards to family history and stories, be kind, sympathetic, empathetic, and, most of all, be funny.

My mom helped in the office at Saint John Vianney Grade School, and this is the school picture, not a mug shot, from about 1958 or so. Don't let her charming smile fool you. Behind this happy countenance was the woman my brothers and I called "Mom."

Chapter Five

The Garage

In the Village of Ars, my folks' garage was attached to the house. But like the driveway, which was about two and a half lanes wide in front and to the south side of the garage, it narrowed to one lane halfway down the drive toward the street. So, the garage was more than a single stall but not really a full double stall either. Maybe it was all the crap we had on both sides of the garage that shrunk it. It was always full of stuff. Some of it was my dad's, and some of it was ours, like bikes, wagons, boxes full of baseballs and gloves, bats, footballs, and barbells. But there was a lot of other crap, too. The lawn mower, rakes, hoses, and the garden stuff like hoes and shovels were stuffed in there in spite of the fact that we had a shelter house at the back of the lot for just such items. There were usually large sacks of potatoes and onions and, occasionally, a mesh bag of oranges or grapefruits, a gift from Uncle Joe and Aunt Marge, just outside of the door between the house and the garage.

In the summer, we could park the car outside, and the young ones could play in the garage during rain while the elders lifted weights with our friends. It was like a playground gym. Besides also being a car park, it had other functions as well. One that was memorable was that it was the Schlosser Coliseum. Many a spectacle took place there.

The door from the house came down two steps into the garage, and it was pretty much permanently open, even on mild winter days. My mother's ironing station was strategically positioned between the kitchen and the living room, yet a step away from the vestibule and front door as well as the breakfast nook and the door leading to the garage. From this command post, Mom could survey the goings on by the TV in the living room and register who was going into a bedroom or bathroom. She could guard the front door (None of us boys could use the front door. "It's just not done," Mom explained. I was in college before I got to use it, and after I was married before I got to use it regularly), and she could observe the space just beyond the back door into the garage to see if any of us were trying to snitch beer which usually occupied the spot under the potatoes, onions, oranges, and grapefruits.

It was like her military post. She manned it day and night when she wasn't fixing a meal, bathing the little ones, or putting them to bed. She was always there, literally, day and night. You really had to be "good" to get away with something with her always watching, always on patrol, perpetually checking up on you. From this spot, she could "survey hers and yours" as she used to say. It was less of an observation than a warning, and we all understood it. In reality, nothing was really ours; everything was really hers. We didn't really have any possessions of our own like clothes, toys, food, or drink, but for the grace of God and His mother's namesake, our mother, Kathyrn Mary. Everything, we included, was there at her discretion. We never doubted this. Bill Crosby used to tell of his father, saying that he brought his son into the world, and he could take him out, and he'd make another one who looked just like him. This was precisely the attitude of my mom. We were all there at her pleasure.

In my junior year of high school, there was a class that was giving me fits. It wasn't so much that the subject of chemistry was all that difficult; rather, it was the fact that the guy teaching it was a horrible teacher. Virtually, everyone taking the subject felt this way. Fortunately, my dad was a pharmacist, and, from an early age, he made my brothers and me aware of the chemical analysis of things. When he was home, he would periodically help us with our homework, and chemistry was his favorite subject. He was actually a much better teacher of it than the guy hired to do so.

Mr. A was a DP from an eastern-European country who was expertly adept at Chemistry, but he couldn't teach it to save his soul. He was good one on one, but three days a week were lectures, with the remaining two days set aside for lab. His lectures were difficult in part because of his accent and mannerisms, not to mention his looking like an old TV character called Mr. Peepers. His lectures were a long fifty minutes. The labs were not long enough. The "brownnosers" (a.k.a. "suck ups") were at the far end of the room, so my end was largely ignored. This meant that nearly anything went from coffee to distilled wood alcohol. Furthermore, I always did well on lab exercises and quizzes. Certainly, the same could not be said for lecture tests, but labs made up for any low test grades. That was what he said at the beginning of the year, but he decided to make an exception because of my shenanigans during lectures and during labs. He marked me down because of discipline. There was a special area on the quarterly grading slip for misbehavior. He always checked that portion and lowered my lab grades, too. Now, this was not fair. What junior in high school keeps all of his lab sheets and quizzes? Certainly, not me. The good Lord and my mother gave me a brain with a mind, and I could remember the scores and their average. But what went in his grade book was deflated because of my screwing around.

The second quarter's grade really pulled my fall semester grade down. I went and talked to him about it.

He sat on his stool in his long lab coat and grinned as he fumbled through his grade book. "Ah, hear you are, Schlosser. Let me see. What did you get? Well, that seems to be correct according to my records."

Well, I told him his records were wrong, and that my dad was coming to see him about the grade. The smirk was gone from his face.

Maybe he had other encounters with Germans, I thought, during the war perhaps. He certainly was not so smug now. The class the next few weeks went better, too; I wasn't screwing around as much, and I let him see that I was keeping my papers and comparing the scoring with other students in the class. Dad, unfortunately, was out of town for another week or two.

When Dad finally went to see Mr. A, he apparently didn't seem to be the overbearing German I imagined Mr. A fearing he would be. Apparently, they got on rather well and agreed that I probably knew my chemistry well enough, but my behavior needed work, and that screwing around in a chemistry lab was putting other "good students at risk of harm," or something to that effect. Hence, my grades sometimes suffered because of that. Hell, my dad is German; he bought into that crap. By the time, Dad was home from the meeting; I was the culprit who was symptomatic of the growing juvenile delinquency in the United States and the erosion of culture, education, and standards as well. That was not only a useless meeting; it was detrimental to my well-being. What a waste.

My mom would never have sold out and joined the enemy. My dad always made my mom look good in situations like this. It justified in my eyes Dad's taking the rap for "the chair."

Mom and Dad in 1943
Again, do not be fooled by her sweet appearance; for although she was my mom, I also knew she was lethal. On the other hand, my dad hardly looked threatening to any of the Axis foes.

In the spring, the third quarter grades were done. I had kept my tests, my quizzes, and lab sheets; so, I was ready. Dad had been gone for weeks, and things had gotten a little wild, both at home and at school. The neighbor girl I was dating was giving me grief. We were a pretty steady thing, but she would go out to some of the big school dances with seniors. She did this starting in our sophomore year. I was stupid and put up with it. There was nothing serious. We went to Catholic schools and took stuff like serious dating "seriously." The serious stuff would have to wait until later, much later. Public schools girls might be different, but my brothers and my friends thought, like I did, that Catholic girls were different. As I said before, I was stupid. It was that parochial upbringing in the Village of Ars as well as the whole Catholic school thing. But that's another story for another time.

In each class, students received their individual grade slip from the instructor. Since parents paid something toward tuition, it was assumed their little darlings would bring home the grades. As Mr. A handed me the grade slip, that annoying little smirk appeared on his face.

I looked down and followed across the grading line: first quarter, second quarter, average for the first half of the year. Then, for the third quarter, there it was again, and adjusted grade largely based on the last couple of weeks behavior. I just stood there and looked up from the sheet and glared at him. I crumpled it up, threw it at him, and said, "That may be my discipline grade, but it's not my chemistry grade, you little prick."

No one said a word. Mr. A's face showed concern, but it passed as he came to see that I was not going to do anything else, especially of a violent nature, especially to him. His smirk didn't return, but I knew my "ass was grass" as we used to say. By the end of the day, I was expelled for a week. At the end of the week, I could expect a meeting with Mr. A, the assistant principal, Father M. (a "real dick" as we also used to say), my parents, and, possibly, me. But that was a week away. The immediate problem was where I was going to hide out all day, every day, during school hours, and not draw attention to myself and not get into more trouble. You see, I wasn't going to tell my mom. For some reason, it did not dawn on me that maybe the school would phone her and inform her of the day's events.

I hitchhiked home a little later than usual. I cut across the front yard, went around the garage, came in the backdoor, and totally concentrating on what I was going to say, or not say, to my mom. I did not register that the door between the garage and the house was closed. It was never closed. Well, never, unless there was an ambush in play. There was just such an ambush awaiting me. The garage light went on; the back garage door slammed shut. The door between the garage and the house swung open and the "fans" at the coliseum, my brothers, files out to cheer the events.

There she was, scowling, and holding a baseball bat. This was the accepted fare. Another one of my uncles, also named Ted, Mom's brother, pitched in the Dodger organization. Baseball was not only the national pastime; it was my mother's side of the family's sport of choice. We had baseballs, gloves, and bats aplenty. When the boys got older, the traditional ways of beating us proved insufficient. Mom was getting older, and we were getting bigger.

So, the new deal she decided on (it was not negotiated) involved her usage of a bat with the stipulation she would not use it above the elbows. There was no negotiation, discussion, or counterproposals to this rule. It was her rule, and she ruled.

I immediately dropped the books and started to circle away from her as if she were some dangerous game or predator or beast in the arena. My brothers had chosen sides. Some were rooting for Mom while others were for me. No one was neutral. Those against me had suffered some indiscretion from me as of late. It may have been me getting the last morsel of food that had been especially good, or it could have been me dominating the TV program choices. Who knew? It was not permanent. My brothers and I had no permanent grudges. Everyone was flexible. Sometimes, one would change sides in the middle of a contest. I mean, everyone was on Mom's side in the great totality of things. But on the small things, at any given moment, we would cheer for an underdog for example. Mom didn't mind; it just pissed her off even more, and she liked it that way.

After all the "sons," Mom was so pleased to have a granddaughter. This grandmother was not the "mother" my brothers and I remembered. All of us boys gave her granddaughters, and she loved us for it and spoiled the girls the way she never did us boys.

To return to the story, we were circling each other. I didn't pay any attention to the din of the crowd, the "great unwashed," the shouts of my brothers. Then, she grabbed my shirt, and I started running in a circle. The object was twofold: stay ahead of her swing and also to get her dizzy. Things were going well as we wheeled around the coliseum, and I believe she was both tiring and getting dizzy when it happened. Momentum twisted me so that my right hip was exposed and whirled me to the left. She had my left sleeve, and my right hip was there for the blow. She had caught me on the butt a couple of times, and that brought a roar from the crowd, but no damage and no pain. I had enough padding in my ass to prevent disaster.

My exposed hip was another matter. Her blow landed directly on my right hip. The pain, more than the strike, dropped me in my tracks. I gritted my teeth and went down hard. My brothers instinctively knew I was hurt, and I was not faking it. Fortunately, so did Mom. She dropped the bat and immediately knelt down next to me to comfort and help me. All I could muster was, "Oh Mom, you really hurt me." It was the only hip pointer I ever had in all the years of sports I had played. It came from my mom, in the garage, in front of my brothers, for getting thrown out of school.

You know, I don't remember much about the rest of the week, except that I stayed at home to recuperate. I couldn't go to school anyway. She never said a thing about getting thrown out of school. When it came time for my folks to come down to school to discuss the dismissal, Mom went alone. Dad wasn't home yet. Relatives of the assistant principal, Father M., lived around the corner, so Mom obviously worked that angle. She stood up for me and fought for me against the chemistry teacher, Mr. A. It was obvious she didn't like him. I had given her all the tests, quizzes, and lab papers establishing what my grade average should have been. With this paper trail, she flaunted the evidence in front of Mr. A's face and reverently placed them in front of the priest.

The principal, Father Y., was called in and shown the evidence, but he supported Mr. A. as a wonderful teacher and addition to the staff. "We are very fortunate to have him," Father Y. stated.

Later, Mom told me Mr. A. acted like an "English landlord," and Father Y. was like a "British Major." The principal, Father Y., had been a chaplain in the United States Army and had an authoritarian "Upper" swagger. Needless to say, she liked neither of them.

But I was back in, and she never told my dad as far as I ever knew. It was between us. Like the ball bat and my hip pointer, mum was the word. What went on in the arena stayed in the garage. I never ever remember my mom saying, "You wait till your father gets home. I'm telling him everything. Then, you are going to get it." No. No. No. She ran the camp, she was the disciplinarian, and she meted out justice.

The episode was done, over, finished. Mr. A. did not want to deal with my mom, and it was apparent that I would go to my mom in the future if there were any incidents that I felt were unfair. It was also that Father M. was influenced by my mom. Later, I found out he was half Irish. Maybe that accounted for some of it, too. I do not know. All I knew for sure was that Mom was better in such situations than my dad was. She was better in many situations. We liked Mom best.

Years later, when she was suffering from dementia, I would get out to the house a couple of times a week, and I would find her sitting alone across the living room from her old post. We would talk for hours. Mostly, it was her asking me if I wanted a cup of coffee. I've never drank coffee regularly, and never in front of her. But she would ask me if I wanted some about every ten minutes. I never got upset with her asking; I'd either say, "No, I'm full," or "Oh, I've had enough. I'll have to sleep in the tub tonight." That always brought a smile to her face. She used to say that, probably an old Irish saying.

Eventually, my dad would show up. He went to mass every morning across the street at Saint John's. He would stay for doughnuts or he would go to the store for something. I was always concerned about him leaving Mom alone now, even for an hour. No one knew what she might do. She never did wander off.

He confided in me that he just had to get away once in a while. "She's driving me nuts by asking if I want a cup of coffee. Hell, I've never drank coffee. When I married her, I had all the coffee-Coffey I ever wanted," Dad said. Coffee-Coffey, it was his wittiest pun. But I understood. Twenty-four hours a day with Mom the way she was was a long day. Deep down, I had suspicions that she was up to something because every now and then, I would notice a glint in her eyes as if to say she was only faking some of her troubles and was simply playing with us, to get even, to let us know she could still "drive us to drink" as she used to say.

Then, there were other days she was penitent over something she had instigated long ago. She remembered some seemingly long-forgotten incident which rekindled in me the notion that she not only had all her marbles, but that she was still "sharp as a tack." One day, as we sat there, she said, "Do you remember that time I had you go out back and cut a switch so I could switch you? I gave you a couple of good whacks, and then told you to 'go back out in the backyard and cut another one; this one wasn't good enough.' You did it, and I really hit you with it. I shouldn't have done that. I really hit you. I should not have done that to you."

I laughed a little and said, "Hell, I don't remember that. It must not have been too bad because I don't remember it." But, in fact, I did remember it. It was one of the worst switchings I ever got, and the back of my legs had whelps and hurt for days. I remembered that one, but for the life of me, I cannot remember what I did to deserve it. Interestingly, the one I would have liked to mention to her with a laugh was the ball bat episode in the garage. Maybe I remember that one more vividly because I was older and I was laid up for a couple of days after that particular whipping.

But Mom was old now. So, I denied the one and didn't mention the other. With the advantage of years, I can laugh about both of them. But the one she mentioned and remembered vividly must have brought anguish to my mom during all those long fifty some years. I hope my lie calmed her conscience. I have no doubt I deserved it, and sending me out for a better one was part of the psychology of parenting back then. I hope my kids lie to me when I ask them if they remember some of the dumb things I did to them, and meekly say, "I shouldn't have done that," asking for their forgiveness. The difference is that I really don't deserve it, and Mom did. She had her hands full with all of us boys. In hindsight, I think she was a saint going into our family and a saint going out of it.

My mom and I are at my eldest son's wedding. She was almost ninety, and I was still trying to get even with her for sixty years of past episodes.

Chapter Six

The Iron

During my eighth grade year at Saint John Vianney Grade School in the Village of Ars, it became known that about five of the graduating classes were not going to go downtown to Catholic Central. This news made me pause. There had been kids from grades above me who went on to high school at the public schools, but, I guess, I didn't pay attention to that or I just dismissed it. For whatever reason, classmates of mine, from my graduating class, not going on to Catholic Central was disturbing.

Most of us had been together for years. We had been confirmed together, made our first confession and first communion together, and had gone to mass every day before classes for years together. So, the news that some were not going to Catholic Central was a shock. I wondered, *How come?*

This was in the spring of 1959, and when I went home for lunch, I asked my mom, "How come?" I need to explain that the Village of Ars was pretty parochial, to say the least, but my family was in many ways much more so. Mom had taught us boys the rudimentary history of both Ireland and the Catholic Church. We got some Church history at school, but Mom's instruction was of a higher level and with deeper insights. As contradictory as this sounds, Mom knew stuff they didn't teach in school. All my brothers and I knew this. The way she told the stories, she had been there for much of the happenings, or family members had been there. There was a lot of stuff she knew that was general knowledge, but she knew her stuff on a level that was close to being omniscient and sacred.

She had explained how the Brits had allowed Protestants to establish their own schools in Ireland and England that were called "public" schools. Catholics had their Catholic schools, and Protestants had their "public" schools. She overlooked pointing out that "public" in the United States did not mean Protestant. We had no problems with Protestants; half of our families were Protestants. My dad's mom was from a Protestant family, and my mom's dad was from a Protestant family. So, we had grandparents who were Protestant, uncles and aunts who were Protestant, and cousins who were Protestants. My Protestant cousins went to "public" schools, and the Catholic ones went to Catholic schools. It was just that simple and obvious.

Armed with factual analysis that Catholics went to Catholic schools and Protestants went to "public" schools, I was blinded, or blindsided by another important point: Mom didn't explain that there was a difference between British "public" schools and American "public" schools. So, when I asked why some of my Catholic grade school classmates were going to the "public" Protestant schools, I was reflecting on my ignorance of the facts.

What was to compound the issue was that when I asked my mom why they were going to "their" (Protestant) schools, she did not clear up the confusion; rather, she compounded it. She retorted, "'Tis a shame." I thought that it truly was a shame from two points of view: on the one hand, it was obvious that the families of my ignorant classmates did not know or understand the Protestant nature of "public" schools and were, thus, subjecting their children to a confusing situation; on the other hand, my former classmates were not going to attend "our" (Catholic) schools and, thus, be in the proper place in the nature of things.

You see, we had Protestant relatives and friends, but they were excused from discrimination because they were "our Protestants." On the other hand, Protestants who were strangers, well, they were Protestants with a capital "P." They were the "them" in the equation of "us versus them." As to my classmates who were going to "their" schools with "them," well, what was to be said? It was obvious that these people did not enjoy the knowledge, understanding, and wisdom that only my mother possessed concerning such matters. Being deprived of her infinite insights, they were doomed to commit error upon error. It was a pity.

I was in high school before someone explained the truth to me. Catholic grade schools went through eighth grade, and Catholic high schools went from ninth through twelfth; none of the junior high or middle school foolishness. It was about my sophomore year when somebody explained to me that "public" did not mean "Protestant." At first, I didn't believe it, but then, a good friend explained it to me. Interestingly enough, though armed with this new knowledge, I never once questioned the source of my misunderstanding. I never once questioned what my mom had taught us about this or any other subject. I had learned a long time before that it was just better left alone. She had her reasons for what she said and did, and if we didn't get it, it was too bad for us.

Now, a friend of mine who lived next door to our family in the Village of Ars went to the local public school. He started at Catholic Central but transferred after his freshman year. This set of circumstances strained our relationship over the rest of our high school years and beyond, I think. But, in our senior year, I was coming home from school one afternoon, and he was heading out. We stopped to talk for a few minutes in the adjoining front yards. He said he was training for the Golden Gloves and that why don't I swing around some time to check it out. I had friends who had fought in the Gloves, but I didn't know anyone from the Cassard Post, which was about a mile and a half away in the Home Acres area of Division Avenue. I didn't follow him up on the invite, but, a week or two later, I ran into him again, and he said he was scheduled to fight this coming Saturday night in the Light Heavyweight Novice Division. He said, "Hey, all you CC (Catholic Central) boys lift weights and are 'bad asses.' Why don't you register to fight for us at the Cassard Post? We don't have anybody in Novice Heavyweight class."

I have no idea what the hell was running through my head, but I said, "Okay. Get the papers for me. I'll forge my folks' signature." Everyone in the Golden Gloves had been preparing for months for the actual fights. I'd never had gloves on, sparred, or been in an actual ring. Novice my foot, I was a virgin with more guts than brains. I'd been in fights all through high school, down at school and in the neighborhood, but nothing formal. I guess I just wasn't going to let my neighbor think that us, "bad asses" from CC, wouldn't step up on a moment's notice and couldn't do the impossible.

On Friday night, I forged the papers, and on Saturday, I, too, was scheduled to fight Novice Division Heavyweight for the Cassard Post. My neighbor instructed me not to eat any fatty foods prior to the bout, and to eat at about 3:00 or 3:30 P.M. on Saturday. Well, we didn't eat until 5:30 P.M. on Saturday, and we always had hamburgers and potato chips. I think the neighbor specifically mentioned that these two foods should be avoided. I couldn't sidestep the usual Saturday meal without bringing all sorts of attention to myself. So, I ate my usual couple of burgers and chips between 5:30 and 6:00 in the late afternoon. A friend who was wise to the affair picked me up, and off we went, as innocent as the day to the fights.

I drew a "by" on the first fight, so I didn't fight until late, about 10:30 or so. When I mounted the steps leading into the ring, I saw my corner man for the first time, and I noticed all the blood droplets on the mat. But things were rushing now, and time was flying.

All I remember was that my corner man, a black guy, about fifty years old, told me, "He's a south paw, a lefty. He'll come at you backwards. Fight him accordingly."

I thought, *Backwards? What the hell does that mean?*

As I looked across the ring, all I remember was that he had what seemed to be a foot in height on me, which also meant his reach was also in his favor. The bell rang, and he was over in my corner and intent on killing me. He was from a farming area outside of Grand Rapids, and I suspect was Dutch for some reason. Putting away a Catholic city boy would be a feather in his cap. I could just imagine him strutting like a bandy rooster.

All I remember was that I was hunched low because I had just turned around in my corner, and I threw a couple of low combinations, and then, I straightened up and followed with a right cross. He went down like a tree, as if I had planned it, drawn it up, and had practiced it. What was even better was that he didn't get up.

I had a problem, though. Years earlier, I had blown my right knee while playing football. I would like to think it was the reason, virtually, that no colleges and universities seriously looked at me with scholarships. I was seeing a doctor about reconstructive surgery. It so happened that the doctor was the ringside physician, and he nearly stopped the fight before it began because he was well aware of my injury and the severity of it. But, he let it go on. The problem now was that I had blown it out again as I hit my opponent and was standing in the ring on one leg and couldn't get to a corner.

I sort of hopped to a corner; my opponent was counted out, and the doctor went to help him while my corner man rushed up to me, gave me a hug, and called me "champ."

Things were still happening fast, and amid the wild cheering, I could hear the doctor say, "Where's your mouthpiece? You didn't swallow it, did you?" He had real concern on his face.

"I didn't have one," I answered.

He put his hand to his brow and shook his head and exhaled loudly.

I had had "the luck of the Irish." I was helped down from the ring into the waiting arms of my friend who was laughing and congratulating me all at once. "I knew you'd do it," he said over and over.

All I could say was, "Shit, my folk, my mom, is going to kill me."

My neighbor's dad and brother were at the fights and called my folks to congratulate them on having a "champ" for a son. By the time I got home, about midnight, my folks were both waiting up for me. There was no congratulatory salutation. I don't remember them saying anything actually. I just went off to bed. The next morning, the *Grand Rapids Press* carried the stories of the Golden Gloves bouts, and the winners had their pictures there, too. The phone rang off the wall for days. I could tell my mom was proud of me, and Dad was, too, I suppose. Neither said anything to me, but I heard their conversations when they didn't think I would hear them, and they were both proud, especially Mom.

With my knee torn up, I could not continue to the next level of fights. My neighbor was my replacement. He put on about six pounds with the help of hamburgers, chips, and milk shakes. He took the state title.

This is my picture from the *Grand Rapids Press* after winning
the Novice Heavyweight Division of the
Golden Gloves in 1963.

I had no intention of going back in the ring again, at least for a while. But a funny thing happened. Some friends who fought out of the West Side Youth Center let it be known that Gloves fighters were welcome to put on bouts at various clubs, like the Am Vets and American Legion, in small towns around Grand

Rapids such as Lowell, Belding, Newago, Freemont, Ravenna, Allegan, and Ionia. The pay was five dollars a fight, and maybe a beer if they thought you could handle it. Gas for the car was twenty-nine cents a gallon, so the opportunity to make money and get a beer or two was too good to pass up.

Every Saturday night, there was a road trip to a fight. It was all rigged. We would agree ahead of time who would win and who'd take a dive. The pay was the same, so it was all the same to us. There were usually four of us, sometimes six. So, it was all set before we got there.

We would put on a good show and exhibit some awesome theatrics. We were using sixteen-ounce gloves. By the second round, our arms were so tired; we really had to get in close and fake some severe body punches. Then, we'd part and one of us would land a loud slap to the upper chest of the opponent. He'd throw his head back as if it was the recipient of a devastating blow to the chin and keel over backward on the mat. It looked real enough, and we got paid, and our whistles were wet, and life was good.

The only time it got out of hand was when a local hayseed wanted to fight. Not outside after the bout, but he wanted a match against one of us. This was never good because his girlfriend, mom and dad, cousins, uncles and aunts, friends and neighbors, and dog were all there cheering him on, and he really couldn't lose in front of all of them. This was suggested a few times, and the answer was always, "No, our insurance didn't cover anyone but us." We didn't have any insurance; we just didn't want to fight any local hick.

But, this one night, the offer was sweetened by "another ten bucks" to take on Jethro or whoever, for three rounds. Well, ten bucks was a lot of money back then, so I said, "Okay." He was a big corn-fed boy who probably threw bales of hay up in the barn loft for hours at a time. He was really big. Sure enough, he was there with his whole entourage. I was having second thoughts when an inner voice whispered, *They think city slickers are pussies.* It was a matter of pride now.

I wore a brace on my knee now, but thought I might try to fit it to my neck because this guy looked really, really, *big*. One of my friends advised, "Stay away from him. Move around and tire him out."

I thought, *The only way this guy was going to tire out was if I could get him to run and chase me as I drove the car around the county.* The bell rang, and my five supporters were drowned out by his fifty human fans and his one four-legged fan. It was taking on the appearance of a rodeo.

I kept away from him as best I could. I think I put about a mile on my shoes during the first round alone. As I looked across at him in his corner in-between rounds, I saw he was swearing.

Somebody in my corner said, "We've got him now."

As I turned to look incredulously at who offered that comment, the bell announced round two. I immediately went for the neutral corner to my right. As I did so, he relaxed as he started to stalk me, and I turned and blasted him. Not once, or twice, but three punishing blows to the head. He was dazed and went down. I never took my eyes off of him. He was on all fours and shaking his head. He was clearly stunned. The ref had not cleared away from him when I shot past the ref and blasted the big man before he knew what hit him. He was back on all fours, and the thought entered my mind of jumping on his back and putting on a real rodeo, but I thought better of it.

The ref was yelling at me, and I just pummeled the poor stunned animal. If I had had a branding iron, I would have gone to work on that doggie. As it was, he was really out of it and confused.

I had a mouthpiece this time, so I mumbled to the ref, "End it." You would have thought I had asked if we could fly a Soviet hammer and sickle flag over the courthouse.

He said in a disgusted voice, "Hell no."

Before I could pull off another sneak attack, the round ended. The folks at the ringside looked decidedly upset. The city kid was handling their boy, and they were in a foul mood. What added insult to injury was the sneaky way I had punished their man. I suppose the wise thing might have been to take a dive and let him win. But, there was no way I was going to let him tag me so I could throw this fight. I was trying to figure out a way that I could hit Jethro and the ref. Both of these guys were getting on my nerves. I told my corner to, "Drift outside after the fight and start the car; have it pointed toward Grand Rapids."

On the third round, I was willing to box the big man because he was clearly leery of me. He was no boxer. He was a brawler. His arms were getting heavy, but those gloves covered very dangerous fists. I could spar with him now, get in close, and throw some actual boxing combinations. There was blood coming from his nose, but I needed to end this thing. So, I resorted to an old dirty trick. I shot a left jab past his head and dragged the laces of the glove across his right ear, cutting and tearing it some. I did it again, and he could not only feel the pain, but he could see his blood on my glove. As he intently stared at my left glove, I landed a series of rights that had him on the mat again. I motioned to the ref to end it.

He ignored it.

So, I spit my mouthpiece out and yelled at the wounded beast, "Stay down. Come on, ref, do your job. I'm going to tear him up, rip his ear off, and beat him to a pulp."

The ref finally did the right thing, and called him out.

Was I glad, I was standing there with all my teeth and no mouthpiece. I immediately helped the stud up, said loud enough for his fans to hear, "You are the toughest fight I've ever had. I'm glad the ref ended it. You would have probably come back and kicked my ass. How about a rematch next month?"

He mustered a "Yeah, okay."

I thought, *Not on your life. Next time, you'd kill me. I'm quitting while I'm ahead with ten dollars to boot. I'm out of here for good.*

With a blink of an eye, I got my money, said I'd be in touch for a rematch, and I headed for the door. I grabbed about six beers off the counter on the way out. The car was running and heading to Grand Rapids. Five miles down the road, it was obvious we were not being followed.

All I could muster was, "Shit, what a night. We ain't doing that again. I don't care how much they offer."

About three weeks later, "the crew," as we called ourselves, showed up at the house to pick me up. We were headed out somewhere. It was not to a fight. My mom was at her station in the doorway between the kitchen and the living room, ironing clothes, when the gang showed up at the front door. I went by her, absorbing her stare. It was obvious they weren't going around to the back door of the house. It was dark. No one would hear them banging back there, and every other guy was collected at their front door.

They all crowded in the vestibule and were very polite to my mom. They had heard the stories. A few of them had witnessed her in action and seen her handy work. Their demeanor was based on fear, not so much on etiquette. I said I'd be back home about midnight or so.

Mom said, "You guys are going out fighting again, aren't you?"

Like a chorus, we all answered, "No, no. We are done with that stuff."

I said, "No, Mom, honest, not tonight."

She turned and stood her iron on the ironing board. No one had started out the door yet when she rounded on me and said, "You want to fight? Fight me."

I turned slightly away from the crew and toward my mom, and she landed a left jab right on my chin. Then, she used her right to punch me in the gut.

I said kiddingly, "All right, you want to fight?" I just stuck my left out, and she walked right into it. It staggered and startled her. I didn't really hit her. She walked into it. Time stopped, everything was frozen, and nothing moved. The gang just watched openmouthed. She shook it off and looked as if she was going to fall backwards. I took a couple of steps toward her, trying to grab her to prevent her fall when she wheeled around, grabbed the plugged-in iron, and tagged me with it on the left side of my face. Part of my left eyebrow was singed off, and the red gothic-shaped window design from the iron was pressed onto my face. My cheekbone and the bone at the outer corner of my eye throbbed. Tears came to my eyes as I covered my face with my hands.

All I could muster was, "Mom!"

I heard the commotion, and then peeked a look as five asses and ten legs squeezed through the front door all at one time amid shrieks of terror.

"She hit him with an iron," said one emerging into the safety of the front yard.

Another added, "And it was plugged in."

Someone else asked, "Jesus, is he okay? Is he dead?"

I was vaguely aware of the commotion in the front yard when I saw my mom starting to lean over me. Was she coming in to land more damage? I did not notice that she had again placed the iron on the ironing board. So, this time, I struck. I landed one right on her jaw from my prone position on the tile floor, and then, I, too, was through the door, into the front yard. We all piled into the car and were gone before she could kill the lot of us.

I said, "Damn. You believe that shit?"

To a man, they all answered as one, "No way." Everyone was awestruck. I didn't go home for about a week. I stayed at a friend's house whose parents couldn't believe the tale we told. They found it difficult to believe no matter how many times we told it, never varying the story. It was emblazoned on our collective consciousness and on the side of my face. My buddy's parents negotiated a truce and a safe conduct guarantee for my return home. Again, nothing was said about this incident then, or later, by my mom. In a couple of weeks, the telltale gothic point on the side of my face disappeared, too, so it was over. Just like that. I would occasionally bring it up, only to receive a stare and threatening look as if to say, "It can happen again." No, thank you. Once was enough.

My gothic design lasted about two weeks. When asked about it, I would retort that I was considering going into the church, that I had "my eye on a church position," maybe a Dominican priest. The teachers and clergy at Catholic Central were dubious about my vocation claim. They probably thought it was some prank gone wrong, and that I deserved the blemish for doing something unsavory. Actually, no one believed any of the stories told about it, the real story or the fakes, certainly, not my clerical-calling story.

Well, maybe for just an instant, you never knew, but maybe not. No, probably not. Actually, none of the neighbors believed that vocation story for a minute. My friends told the actual story every now and then, sometimes adding embellishments. It needed no exaggeration. It could stand by itself as one hell of a story.

We were not void of religiosity. My best friend decided to give up his girl friend for lent. He was still quite fond of her, but, after forty days, he was cured of her, and she of him. It wasn't a religious calling; it was more of a religious negation. I wish I had done it with the girl I was dating back then. But I wasn't religious at all.

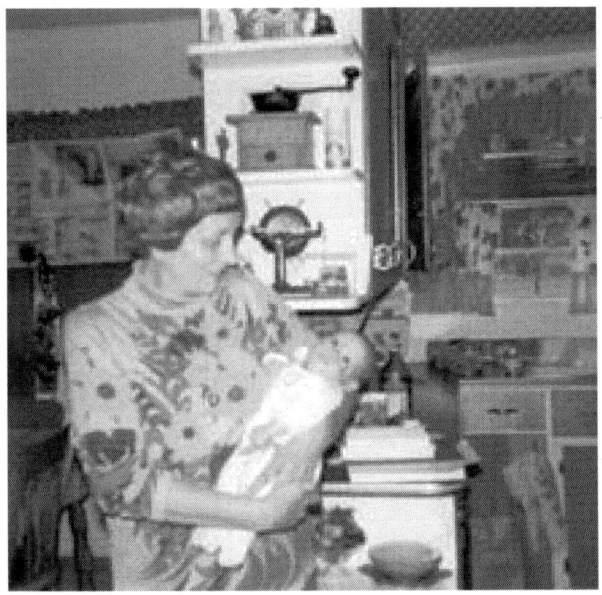

Mom with my oldest daughter, Amy; I know it is difficult to imagine this gentle, kind, loving soul coming after me with an iron, but the fact of the matter was, she did, and I'm amazed I turned out somewhat normal.

My eyebrow eventually grew back. "The crew" talked about that episode for weeks—no, months on end. They would have kept it up, but high school was coming to an end, and many of us would go our merry way with new adventures to spark our interest.

One immediately comes to mind. About a month after returning home from high school, I was awakened by the most realistic dream I've ever had. Somebody was beating me to a pulp, but I couldn't see who. There was laughing and cheering in the background. And it was all so real. I came to I realize I wasn't dreaming it because it was really happening to me.

My mom had tied my arms and legs to the bed frame, and she was sitting on me, just slapping and punching me and saying, "Mr. Tough Guy, huh? So, you hit women, huh? Not so tough now."

It was obvious she was kidding around, but the pain was real enough. My brothers were crowded into the room, egging her on. It lasted about ten minutes longer. Hell, there were tears in my eyes. She really landed a few. I couldn't believe it. My mom beat me up after tying me to the bed. What a mom!

Mom in 1963, my senior year at Grand Rapids Catholic Central High School and the year of some of our famous bouts

Chapter Seven

Oatmeal/Haferschleim

I do not like oatmeal. I do not remember ever liking oatmeal. The very name conjures up bad memories and leaves a bad taste in my mouth. My wife likes oatmeal, as do my children and my grandchildren. I think there is something wrong with them. For years, I explained the problem with oatmeal, and they persisted in their defiance of my wishes to deny oatmeal an existence. At best, I can tolerate oatmeal cookies, and this is the only form of oatmeal that should be allowed to exist.

When my wife and I would drive our brood down to Florida, out to California, over to Montreal and Quebec, I ate breakfast bars, and my family consumed Styrofoam bowls of instant oatmeal. I often retreated to the car park of the motel so as not to watch my spouse and children eat the stuff. My wife still has it five days a week for breakfast before she heads off to teach. "Cholesterol," she explains. Cholesterol my foot, she does it to see if I, like my dad, can get the dry heaves, get nauseated, and possibly barf. I generally have an iron stomach for delicate situations like cleaning up throw up, messy diapers, and dog piss and shit. But oatmeal brings me to the brink.

Before I explain my aversion, no, disgust, no, hatred of oatmeal, I will explain the only good thing about oatmeal that I could gleam from the first forty years of my life. Then, I'll explain the source of my repulsion for oatmeal.

I began my masters of art through a Western Michigan University program as a student at the University College at Cardiff, Wales. I had applied for study abroad, and, being accepted, I then had to choose a school in the United Kingdom. On hearing the good news from one of my professors, I rushed over to my future wife's dorm to relay the news. I thought it was "good news" going to school abroad, but I wasn't sure how she would take it. Not only was she supportive of it, but she also got her dorm director to let her leave school for the night to drive back to Grand Rapids with me to talk to my folks about going abroad in the fall.

I borrowed a friend's car, and we headed up to Grand Rapids. We had talked a little about possibly getting married during the summer. She was willing to wait. My parents were willing to give me some family financial aid for spending money while on the study abroad.

The only condition and stipulation came from, you guessed it, Mom. "If you choose an English university, you're out of the family," she explained and promised all at once.

Until that point, it was easier than I thought it would be. But now, Mom had spoken.

Quickly looking over the list, I spotted University College, located in a suitably Celtic country, Wales, just across the Irish Sea from Ireland, still known to speak a Celtic dialect of Gaelic. It was a Celtic school to be sure. Gaelic to the bone, I assured her. The deal was struck. I'd go to Cardiff, the most English of Welsh cities and attend the most English of Welsh colleges and universities in Wales, and none would be the wiser. In later years, I thought she may have known this all along, but pretended not to know, letting me think I'd gotten away with one. My older brother was dead by now, and I was the number one son. I was thoroughly Gaelic to her satisfaction. So, I suspect, Mom appreciated a little blarney on my part. You couldn't get much past my mom.

There were about twenty foreign students at University College that year. I used weekends to travel around the western shires of England and most of Wales. Three, four, or five other exchange students chipped in on the car rental and gas. I was the oldest and did not fear driving on the wrong side of the road. None of us had classes on Fridays, so we usually headed out early on a Friday, returning on Sunday. We saw a lot. By Christmas break, everyone from the European continent was heading home, as I also hoped to do. But home would have to wait; my folks sent me a Euro Rail Pass. I had some letters of introduction from professors in the United States of America and at Cardiff, so I decided to visit several monasteries. I was studying the medieval period of history, and this was a great opportunity to visit key institutions dating from the Middle Ages.

I had already visited Prinish Abbey not far from the city of Bristol in England. It was a working Benedictine house with a small but dedicated community of brothers. And now, at Christmas time, I would visit four cloistered communities on the continent. In France, I went to Citeau and Cluny. If you will recall, my dad worked for a Swiss firm, which I also intended to visit, so I also stopped at the famous monastery of St. Gall. The views were heavenly, and the name belies the Celtic foundation of the place. Mom would appreciate my stories of St. Gall.

The last monastery I visited was at Fulda, near the artificial but real border between East and West Germany. Not far away was a United States military base, which guarded the famous Fulda Gap, which came out of Czechoslovakia and East Germany. It was at Fulda's monastic library that I found things worth staying around for. I got the first two nights' lodging free, as prescribed by the Benedictine Order, but I stayed for a week. I had little to no money. The abbot was kind enough to let me work off my room and board.

I would mop floors and wash windows, and clean around the latrines, usually in the morning, while in the afternoons, I had supervised access to the library. It was just as my professors said it would be: ancient manuscripts, many of which were illuminated. These were priceless works of art, and I treasured every minute I had access to them while I was there. The real academic learning took place amid these treasures. Since I was planning on staying here for about a week, I decided to participate in the monastic hours if it pleased the abbot. It did, so I did. That, too, was a learning process and more than an academic exercise. I was included in the ancient rites of an ancient Christian tradition, which gave me a new perspective on the medieval period as well as our modern age.

While pruning trees in an orchard one morning, I was trying to engage one elderly monk in particular. This man was the real McCoy; that is, the real Brother McCoy. But all he did when I asked him something was to smile and nod and go about his business. At first, I thought it might be a language difficulty. So, I tried to keep it simple. Still, there was no response beyond the smile and nod. By now, I thought the old boy may have been simple. Finally, another brother came over and explained that "Brother Matthew" was not being rude. He waited until Brother Matthew was out of earshot, and he explained his situation.

"Brother Matthew took a vow of silence some years back," he explained. "Besides the vows of poverty, obedience, and chastity, he got permission to observe silence. He vowed to remain silent until there was 'peace on Earth and goodwill among men,'" my young friend explained.

"Well, how long has he been silent? He doesn't even chant the office?" I asked. "He got permission from an abbot for that? How long ago?" I had so many questions that my young "brother" couldn't get a word in edgewise.

He waited for me patiently, smiled, nodded, and said, "He took the vows, according to those who know, on September 1, 1939."

The start of World War II, I thought. *My God, that's a long time.* It was December 1967, nearly thirty years.

"He's never said a word?" I asked incredulously.

My friend answered, "No. I've never heard him say one word."

I thought about that incident a lot over the years and fear that if that poor old monk, Brother Matthew, is still alive, he surely has added forty more years to his silence. If he wasn't exactly happy about his vow, he was certainly content to keep it. That was a lesson in and of itself.

There were several more thought-provoking incidents of this nature that I encountered at Fulda. But the ones I wish to present to you all involve food. I had a fixation on food. There was not enough of it. I lost thirty pounds in three weeks at Christmas time in 1967 while visiting those monasteries. Oh, they fed you all right, but there's food, and there's *food*.

Every morning, after we sang or chanted from the Psalter in the church and attended mass, we headed over to the refractory for breakfast. The hall where we ate was like an old barracks dining hall, but with long tables and benches that ran parallel to each other, with the ability to seat at least twenty-five brothers on each side. At the end of these two rows of tables and benches, another three benches ran at a right angle for the abbot and other monks who had certain positions within the monastery.

Over on one side was a pulpit where a brother dutifully read from some classic, like St. Augustine's *Confessions* or St. Benedict's *Rule for Monks*. There were no radios or televisions, no magazines or newspapers. There was no chatty conversation, no discussion of sports, weather, movies, work, or girlfriends—just monks and solitude, broken by spiritual reading and the smell of food.

As I went through the line, we took trays like one had in basic training in the army. They were stamped metal with indentations to hold various food. It was a combination tray and plate. I immediately thought of the army base down the road a few clicks away and smiled. There was this one big burley monk who ladled out *haferschleim*, or oatmeal. Technically, *haferschleim* is translated as "gruel." But the brothers at Fulda called anything and everything that came in wads of oats, flower, or bread "*haferschleim*."

Now, if you recall, I hate oatmeal, and by any other name, it's still oatmeal. But its German name was so descriptive and rich in its pronunciation; I just loved to say it. As I came down the line, the big brother waited for the request to go to work, and I could not find it in my heart to deny him this pleasure. "*Haferschleim, bitter*," I would say.

His ladle dipped deep into the oversized cauldron and, raising it, contained the largest gob of *haferschleim* you could imagine. He would raise it up and then start the downward motion only to snap or jerk the ladle back up, depositing about ten pounds of *haferschleim* on your tray. There was no indentation capable of holding this amount, so it rested over the entire middle of the tray. The tray nearly buckled under the weight, and you had to hold on to your tray because it could fall. I saw it happen to old pro monks who weren't expecting it or who were preoccupied with something more.... spiritual perhaps. There was and is nothing spiritual about *haferschleim*.

Let me explain, I had no intention of eating the gruel; I just liked ordering it. When I go to Germany today, I always order it with no intention of eating it. It is simply a cool word. Once seated, I would trade my gob of *haferschleim* for something better, and damn near anything is better than *haferschleim*.

One might ask, "Where did this dislike for oatmeal come from?" There was one source, and this sole source was the cause of many likes and dislikes in my brothers' lives as well as my own, and that source was our mother.

When my brothers and I were in the "dog house" for some infraction of the rules, often times, there was an alternative to the switching we got. We would be sent to our room for extended periods of time. When we returned from school, we went to our room. After supper, we went to our room. Except for toilet visits, we were banished to our room. On the weekend, all time between meals and toilet breaks found us in our room. Weekends were the worst of it. Added to this confinement was the diet of oatmeal.

Mom used it as punishment, and we came to associate it with punishment. It was never served hot, or even warm. It was cold. We could not use milk with it. No brown sugar or maple syrup—nothing but cold oatmeal. These large gobs of oatmeal took on a life of their own. When we came home from school, there was a wad of oatmeal in a bowl while the others had sandwiches or soup. If we didn't finish it at lunch, it was waiting for us at supper. We had to finish the bowl before we could have another serving of it for the next meal. It was oatmeal, oatmeal, oatmeal. God, I came to hate the stuff.

Oatmeal was one option my mother used as punishment. The switchings and beatings were another possibility. She would sometimes threaten us with having grandmothers stay with us for a while. We loved our grandmas, both of them. But each, in her own way, was a little funny, if not weird. Grandma Schlosser, a fanatical convert to Catholicism, would line us all up and march us over to church to go to confession at two o'clock on Saturday afternoon. First of all, it was Saturday, and we had a million better things to do than go confess to some priest. For that matter, we probably had been to confession during the week, during school, as part of the religion class. We didn't need it yet. Some of the boys felt that since Grandma S was going to bring us to confession on Saturday, they might just as well do something to make the trip worth it.

We didn't do anything too malicious. We might put a FOR SALE sign in someone's yard if they were gone for a weekend. We'd put dog crap in a bag, throw it on somebody's porch, light it on fire, and ring the doorbell. When they came out to stamp it out, there was a smelly surprise in store for them on the soles of their shoes. Turning sprinklers on in the middle of the night at someone's house was always good for a laugh. We would start out very slowly and increase the volume cautiously so as not to draw attention from the house. Wrapping the sprinkler hoses around a parked car from end to end and from top to bottom was fun, too. If our dislike of a neighbor was a little more intense, we might tie a rope around some of his shrubs and attach the other end to his car bumper. He'd pull out the shrubs before he was aware of anything happening.

A couple of times, we rummaged through the trash dumpster at the local grocery store and got some bones from the meat department. We put them in a cardboard box, wrapped the box in nice wrapping paper, put a note TO MY DEAREST or MY HONEY, and put the box inside the backseat of some neighbor's car which was left unlocked and parked in the driveway. We would pull all kinds of pranks and stuff on Friday nights.

If we didn't like the victims, it got a little more serious, like taking the tires off a parked car or filling the house's basement window wells with water or calling a friend and telling him someone's having a party at so in so's house, and we needed one more "horny" guy. We would tell him we had girls from the public school, and they were hot, ready, and willing to go. We would explain we were one guy short, and if they wanted a "good time," to come on over. We'd explain, "This chick is hot to trot." Since all of us were busy, "if you know what I mean," except for the one girl, "a real looker, and stacked," there was no use in knocking at the door. Nobody would hear it, so they should just come in without knocking and go to the basement where everyone was "doing it," and a certain someone was "waiting for it, if you know what I mean." We'd always call some loser whom we let hang around on the fringe of our group.

We'd have him come to some public school girl's house when we knew her folks were home. These guys would blow in the front door only to be confronted by the man of the house about the time the idiot would be heading down the stairs to the dark basement.

Grandma S had no idea she was encouraging mischief and mayhem, but she was.

When the folks would come home, they'd ask, "Why did you do this or that?"

We'd answer, "Grandma made us do it."

They'd say, "What?"

"She made us all go to confession on Saturday; so, we needed something to confess," we would answer.

Mom understood; she'd just stand there and look at us with sort of a smirk on her face. I think she enjoyed the idea that we gave as much as we received, especially with Grandma S. But Dad never quite got it. Mom understood too well, and we came to understand that she was having Grandma S stay with us on purpose, just to hassle us. It was a form of punishment.

Grandma S was a great cook, and we all loved her meals. She'd fix beef or pork pot roast with the carrots, potatoes, and onions, all done in a big roaster. Her meals were great. But bedtime came at the setting of the sun, which during the school days was way too early to be in the house, let alone getting ready for bed. We'd hide from her, and she'd come after us like a little bulldog, teeth clenched, arms pumping, legs hustling along in her high heels. Those shoes she wore had two inch blocks for heels, and they laced up to her ankles. She was totally focused on catching us. She never did, and we wondered what she would have done if she had caught us. By the time we stopped laughing

Grandma Bessie Schlosser at about ninety years of age, I think
one of my brothers told her this doll was one of his daughters;
another said it was their pet dog, but she wasn't buying it. I
was her favorite because I had the same name as her youngest
son who was killed by an auto while walking to high school.
She used to say he was a "saint," and I was the "opposite."

and surrendered, she was tired and had pretty much forgiven us.
She was okay in most respect, except for confession and bedtime.

Grandma Coffey was something else. She knew what we were
up to most of the time. As long as we were willing to go up to
the store and get her cigarettes, she left us alone. Actually, it was
her meals that concerned us the most. You never knew what to
expect. That old Irish woman ate and fixed some weird crap for
us to eat. For the evening meal, she prepared mushroom soup,
fried liver and onions, kidney pie—stuff that we simply would
not eat under any circumstances. She'd fix asparagus, sweet
potato, and chicken gizzards. Who the hell ate that crap? We expected roast beef, Swiss steak, pot roast, hamburgers, pork chops,

pork roast, baked chicken, fried chicken, baked potatoes, mashed potatoes, corn, wax beans, maybe a head lettuce salad, and cookies, ice cream, cake or rhubarb pie, apple pie, cherry pie, or peach pie. Once in a great while, we had ham and turkey, but that was usually reserved for special occasions like Easter and Thanksgiving and Christmas. My dad taught us that there was enough meat on the outside of animals that you didn't have to eat their innards, and that soup was a midday replacement for solid food.

We had no doubt that Mom put Grandma Coffey up to some of that "Old Sod" cooking and meals just to punish us. One time, in particular, really stands out. It was early fall, and we were just back to school. If you lived within a half-mile radius of school, you had to go home for lunch; few, if any mothers, worked, so it was no big deal.

Grandma Coffey had gone out in the garden and gathered up about a dozen tomatoes, had cut them in half, and then quartered the halves. She put them in boiling water and served it as tomato soup. It was just scalding clear water with chunks of tomato in it. We had never had soup like that, let alone tomato soup looking like that. Tomato soup came out of a can with a paper label saying CAMPBELL'S. We ate the soda crackers, but that soup was not soup, and I sure as hell wasn't going to eat it. She scared most of the boys into eating it, but they were gagging and crying and carrying on something terrible. We, the older ones, were laughing and egging them on. Grandma C "got her Irish up" and cuffed a few of us, threatening to send some of us to Australia and the penal colonies there before most ate it grudgingly, all but me. No way.

The rest returned to school for what was left of recess, but I sat there until it was nearly time for the bell to ring for afternoon classes.

She said, "Go. Come right home after school. You hear me? No dillydallying around. You get home here. If I have to start looking for you, you will get the beating of your life. Do you understand me, Roger Michael?"

I didn't doubt it for a minute. Whenever any of us were in trouble, these Irish women called us by both our given and our baptismal names. I think they were drawing the attention of all our namesakes to our shortcomings. They were shaming us in front of the holy saints. A beating would be condoned and witnessed by saints and sinners alike. She and my mother made sure of it.

After school, I came home, and that bowl of water and tomato chunks were still sitting there. I sat at the table until about nine that night. I do not remember what the rest had for supper, but I didn't get any. I wouldn't get anything else until I ate that soup.

My brothers snuck crackers and apples into the bedroom for me, and I was hungry. When I got up for breakfast, that untouched bowl of soup was sitting there waiting for me. Grandma just looked at me; she didn't say a word. We both knew the rules of a standoff. I headed for school, very hungry, and some of my brothers snuck food for me, which I ate on the other side of the woods where she could not see me.

Lunch came and went as the day before. Buddies in my class had food for me. After school was a repeat of the previous day. I got some food from my brothers that night, which was Wednesday. I went until Friday after school, and then, she made a critical mistake. She left the kitchen for some reason or another. I was out in the backyard with that bowl and emptied it in the neighbor's yard and returned before one could say "Jackie Robinson," who was the fastest baseball player according to my uncle. When Grandma returned, I just stood up and said, "I finished it."

She looked at me through those wire-rimmed glasses, no expression, just a dull stare.

The folks were usually home on Friday night or Saturday, so all was well that ended well. Grandma Coffey knew what happened; she planned it. I think she enjoyed her little perverse games. She also enjoyed teaching us to be belligerent, stubborn, conniving, and conspiratorial. She was Irish. I have no doubt she and my mother had a good laugh as Grandma C told her about the fracas.

My mom had one last punishment involving the depriving of food and the deployment of food. When we were bad, we got oatmeal. But when we were really bad, and my dad wasn't going to be home for a week or more, we were banished to our room. There was no sitting at the table in front of oatmeal. We were in our room every minute we were home. At breakfast, around 7:30 A.M., at noon, and then again about 6:00 P.M., there was a knock at the bedroom door. Upon opening the door, we would find a glass of water and two slices of white bread. Bread and water constituted breakfast, lunch, and supper. Her explanation was quite simple. "This is what they serve in prison, and the way you are acting, you are going to spend time there. So, I'm just preparing you for the rest of your life." Whew! That was brutal. I don't recall what I did, but I was on "bread and water" for three days a couple of times.

Oh, by the way, she was correct because a couple of us spent time in jail at one time or another for varying periods of time. Now, it was jail and not prison, but somehow, that old Irish woman knew. In fact, my first stint in jail was an overnight stay for a prank that went wrong. It was over the Christmas break after high school graduation. We had one guy go into a bar and sit down. About two minutes later, three other guys would rush in, pretend to beat him, drag him out, and throw him in the trunk of the car as we sped off.

The "Purple Gang" was playing at the movies…great inspiration. Our one phone call was to each other's parents, saying their son was staying at someone else's house for the night. The cops caught on and squashed that scheme. Oh, guess what they served us for breakfast? No, not bread and water, but they served oatmeal. Gee, I hate oatmeal, and oatmeal by any other name is still *oatmeal*.

Chapter Eight
The Wake

My wife's family, meaning, her dad and her stepmother, actually weren't thrilled that she was dating me. We met in college. As it turned out, we lived about three miles from each other, but she went to a local public school, Wyoming Park, while I went to Catholic Central, which was located in downtown Grand Rapids. Our paths never crossed during high school. She was also a year and a half younger, hence, a year behind me in school, and that might have entered into the equation as well.

I had recently been dumped for the hundredth time by a neighborhood girl whom I had liked since about fifth grade. She went to a university north of Grand Rapids and cultivated relationships there that did not include me. I should have been wise because she dated other guys, always older, using the excuse that her mother didn't want her to go steady with anyone, and it followed that her mom wanted her to "date lots of guys." This was in high school, so I should not have been so surprised when she let me know her social calendar for her college sophomore year, and I was relegated to some minor time toward the end of some upcoming month.

Deep down, I knew it was coming, but I was stupid and ignorant. Frankly, getting dumped for the last time was not as bad as I thought it was going to be. Of course, her being away at school helped. I saw her rarely thereafter. More importantly, I met my future wife through a friend whom I worked with in a road construction during summer vacation. He knew her from high school and had told her about this handsome, athletic, smart, available guy whom he worked with during summer vacation. The three of us were at college in Grand Rapids, and he had introduced us the first week of school. I was playing football for the college and had broken my collarbone and was looking for sympathy in all the right places. She was a cheerleader as it turned out. She might have witnessed my injury without knowing it was me; just my luck.

But, about a month later, she was hanging posters for Homecoming, and I saw her in the hallway, and I asked her if she needed any help. She said she did. The rest is history, but not the rest of the story. She was good-looking, as she still is. She was athletic, as she still is. She was…well-proportioned, as she still is. She got guys to turn their heads, and she still does.

A friend walked by and asked if I was going to ask her to Homecoming. I was a little embarrassed, had just recently put on the Brown Helmet of being dumped, and was actually not planning on going to the dance. But here was an opportunity to get another Brown Helmet from a complete stranger. She was good-looking, way out of my league, and a cheerleader to boot. There was no way it was going to turn out okay.

I asked anyway. She said, "Yes."

She explained she had a wedding and reception the same weekend as the Homecoming game and dance, but she was sure she could fit it all in. As it turned out, she fitted it all in. I had a great time with her. I'd never dated a well-built, good-looking blond Dutch girl before. But I liked it. I liked all of it.

She worked at a small supermarket between our houses, and the man who ran the meat counter knew my family. She innocently mentioned to the man that she was going to Homecoming with a guy named Rog Schlosser. The man spoke up for the family and said, "He's a Golden Gloves champ."

She OK'd it with her folks, whom I met when I picked her up for the dance and meal. She looked gorgeous. I obviously didn't look so good to her folks, as I was to learn.

I introduced her to my folks, and they fell in love with her. She was the daughter my mom never had. Even my dad liked her, and my dad was partial to the girl I had dated through high school and who had taken to awarding me with Brown Helmets the last couple of years. The blond beauty was named Barb. She was amazing. She ran like a boy. I mean it. She was sort of a tomboy but in a woman's body. My brothers all liked her. My uncles and aunts, cousins, and my high school buddies all liked her. She was a hit with everyone.

I think she was taken with my whole family as much as with me. We dated for the next four years. It was over those four years that her folks and brothers got used to me. I can't say they liked me; I was just always hanging around. And after I graduated with a bachelor of arts and returned from school in Wales, we were seriously talking again about getting married. She had a stepbrother from out East talk to her about marrying a Catholic, and a stepsister from out West talk to her about marrying a Catholic. I could read between the lines, and I knew the talks amounted to suggesting that she consider someone other than a Catholic to marry. While I was going to school in Wales, she attended some religious instruction at the Catholic Information Center in downtown Grand Rapids. When I returned, she said she had a big surprise for me. I was thinking one thing, but her confirmation into the Catholic Church was what she had in mind.

People on both her mother's and her father's side were not pleased. Folks on her stepmother's side were not pleased either. Apparently, we Catholics do not discriminate when it comes to threatening and alienating Protestants. Barb had been baptized and raised a Protestant. Some of these Protestants saw her defection to Catholicism as a Jesuitical conspiracy. I had nothing to do with it, and I don't think the Jesuits or the Dominicans or the Paulists who ran the Catholic Information Center laid a trap for her either.

One evening, I visited her folks before I picked her up from work. I explained our plans about getting married. I also mentioned that the religious question was moot as far as I was concerned. I neither asked her to become Catholic nor did I demanded that she join the Catholic Church. I explained that, in

My beautiful wife, Barb; this was taken in 1981,
and Barb is holding our youngest son, Ted.

fact, I was sort of a "little" Catholic since my paternal grandmother had been a Protestant, and my maternal grandfather had
also been a Protestant. I explained further, I had great grandparents, great-uncles and great-aunts, uncles and aunts, cousins and
friends who were Protestants. My parents had always stressed that
family was thicker than religion, and that "religion was often an
accident of birth." My brothers and I were taught to love the
family, regardless of denomination or religion.

So, although I was raised a Catholic, religion was not an issue.
If Barb wanted to stay a Protestant, it was all right with me. I
was, after all, "just a 'little' Catholic by birth." Her dad weighed
what I had to say, got up, and headed for the door. It was almost

time for me to go get Barb anyway, so I also got up and headed for the door. He had opened it for me.

When I reached it the door, he said to me, ""Look, you are either a Catholic or you are not a Catholic, but you are not just a 'little' Catholic. Somebody is pregnant or they are not pregnant. They are not a 'little' pregnant."

The discussion was over. I might argue with the logic, but I was in no position to argue with her dad, just over two months from the wedding date. I just backed off entirely. Barb handled everything with dignity and grace. There were a few family members who did not grace our marriage with their presence. She never spoke of it to me, but I know she was hurt. A few of her relatives held my religion against her. I was keenly aware of it. But my relatives more than made up for their absence. It was a beautiful wedding, outside the church in a shrine in back of the church building. Her relatives would not have had to even go into a Catholic church. Two friends of ours who were priests officiated at the ceremony. It turned out to be a sunny day, a glorious day, the best day of my life, and I had had some pretty good days.

I was in graduate school and commuting four days a week while she was teaching at the Junior High where she had attended not so many years before. She found a great apartment for us just east of the Grand Rapids city center. It was a second story apartment with a third story ballroom. We lived there until we had our first child—by that time, we needed more room. In fact, I tried to get her pregnant every chance I could just to let her family know they were correct; one is not just a "little" Catholic. And nothing makes you more Catholic than assisting in the conversion of one and the production of a lot more Catholics. As it turned out, I was Catholic, she was a Catholic, and four of her six pregnancies produced four more Catholics. I'm quite certain members of her family hated it and everything about me.

My mother doted over our first born who turned out to be a beautiful little girl who "looked as Irish as Patty's pig." She had dark eyes and hair. She was dainty. We named her Amy Kay. The Kay suited both grandmas since they were both Kathryn and Catherine. Kay was a good compromise. As it turned out, the

Mom and her first granddaughter, my daughter,
Amy Kay; they had a great relationship right till Mom's end.

popular name Amy was the French and, possibly, Irish form of
Emma, my maternal grandmother's name. We did not know that
at the time. This grandma was the Irish one, so I have no idea
how she got the English version of the name, except for the possibility that it sounded American. I will explain this in full in a bit.
It was also my little daughter, Amy, who melted any icy relations,
which might have lingered between her folks and me.

Amy Kay was quite small when she was born. For some
reason, she did not grow the last month of pregnancy. Barb was
cautious and conscientious about everything during the whole
pregnancy. We never could quite figure out what happened. So,
Amy Kay became known as "Little Amy Kay." When she went to
kindergarten, she did not respond to the name Amy Kay
Schlosser. She thought her last name was Kay, her first name
being "Little."

A couple of years later, we were blessed with another little girl
who looked Dutch with her blond hair and blue eyes. A friend
from school wanted us to name her "Alka" which sounded
Swedish, not Dutch. He explained the reason for that name was
that she would be called "Alka Schlosser." I was tempted, but

Barb's better judgment prevailed, and she was named Angela. My folks were incredibly jealous of all the girls coming to my branch of the family. I gave Barb due credit, and also offered that it was to bless me for being such a good boy through childhood. Dad just looked at me, but Mom started across the room for me.

I stopped her with, "Hey, just kidding. We were lucky."

Mom and my youngest daughter, Angie; as you can see, Mom was just thrilled to have all these girls.

We were also blessed with two boys down the road. Tom, the older son, was a terror for Barb.

She always said, "When he turned two, he changed into a daemon. He could look so innocent and cute, but turn your back, and he'd destroy his bedroom by emptying baby powder all over the place. He would take the golf clubs from the garage and beat the car with them. He would break all the basement windows with stones."

All I could offer was, "That's my boy."

Ted was a late surprise, hence, the name Theodore, "God's Gift." I had lots of Teds in the Irish side of the family, and one of my best friends and neighbor was a Ted. It was natural. At the hospital, we agreed that John would be his middle name, or baptismal name.

Amy and Angie, and I'm holding Tom at the Saint Mary's Hospital, visiting Barb the evening she brought Ted into the world.

My older brother was a John, one of my favorite university professors was a John, and a priest friend from our wedding was a John. His weight was okay, but, he was rather short, the doctor said. So, I added a third name, Lothar. Part of the German family came from Alsace and Lorraine between France and Germany. Well, in German, the latter is Lotharingia. So, his third name was Lothar. I figured we would call him "Lo" for short. Get it? "Lo" for short.

Barb got it right away, and said, "Drop it from the birth certificate." I'm pretty sure I did.

Tom has never liked his middle name "Eliot," so all of our kids have issues with their names to one degree or another.

Barb and Ted sharing a private joke

So, at one end of the spectrum, the family was growing, but at the other end, some of the older members were dropping off to the dismay of us all. Many of the Irish family were still living in Upper Canada, and we would go there periodically for reunions of the Quainns, Kellys, Doyles, Mannings, and Coffeys. Rondeau Provincial Park on the north side of Lake Erie and just east of Windsor was the meeting grounds for these gatherings. The Coffey/Doyle clan would go about every ten years or so. One of the stories I heard was that my Coffey relatives were in Canada and were restricted from immigrating to the United States of America. In the mid-'30s, they packed a lunch in a basket and walked over the bridge from Windsor to meet with relatives from Detroit for a picnic.

There was no picnic planned and no lunch in the basket. It contained a change of clothes. They caught a westward-bound train and ended up in Grand Rapids where they stayed with their family, which included my mother. They spent time down in

Hartford, Michigan with relatives there and visited more relatives in Chicago. When I was quite young, I remember going with my grandparents to the Canadian reunion. The road from Grand Rapids to Detroit was two lanes and quite treacherous. I was told to behave and not to distract my grandpa who had to drive the whole way.

At about Lansing, my grandma started drilling me, "If anyone at the border asks where Grandpa was born, you tell them Grand Rapids. This is important, so again, if anyone asks where Grandpa was born…."

On and on, it went. Now, this had to be the late '40s or early '50s, and maybe questions were asked. I never remember ever being asked. But I sure knew the answer I was expected to give.

As my mother-in-law would say, "Things were kind of dicey."

Years later, well after both of my Irish grandparents were long dead, my folks, an uncle and aunt, and a couple of cousins planned to go to a reunion in Canada. I thought it would be a great time. I think Amy was in the sixth or seventh grade, and the rest were old enough to get in touch with their roots. We sent twenty dollars on ahead, about a week before the event, to pay for meat. We were then expected to bring a dish to pass.

We went over on Saturday, spent the night in or around Chatham, and showed up at the park mid-morning for the festivities. The festivities were relegated to finding a parking spot and then finding my folks. More than a thousand showed up on Sunday for the reunion. There were four rows of picnic tables and about thirty tables in each row. People were standing and sitting on the ground; there were so many people. Relatives came from all over the United States of America and Canada, some from Ireland and as far away as Australia.

We planned to start back about three in the afternoon. As I circulated, I noticed large kettles on the end of the rows on the last table, and folks were dropping money into them.

I came back to our preserve and said, "They are collecting money at the end tables."

My naïve father said, "Maybe they need more for the meat. There are a lot of people here."

My mom and I looked at each other and just smiled. Dad and I gave Amy and Angie each a twenty-dollar bill, and off they went to plop them in the kettles.

When the girls came back, I think it was Amy who said, "Do you know what they are collecting for?"

My dad offered his take on it and mentioned, "Meat."

The girls said, "No. It's for the IRA."

My dad turned white. Mom and I just smiled.

I said to my dad, "Don't ask them to go get it back. As a matter of fact, why don't we put more in?"

If the girls, including Barb, were surprised, Dad was horrified. Ah, the Irish. God loves them, and so do I. There are times, though, that I think Mom and I loved them better. She was a great one for sending money to help "the Irish cause" and their "army."

My lovely Dutch wife never said anything that questioned the sanity of my people. But I have no doubt she did have some reservations and questions she would have liked to ask. But she was a trooper. She just went along. No one really expected her to understand. You had to be Irish; she was Dutch, like William of Orange, the victor at the Battle of the Boyne. She had been Protestant and had only recently been initiated into the rigors, mysteries, and traditions of the religious element of being Irish. She was a converted "Orange Woman," in the true sense of the word. It would take years, if ever it were to happen. I planned to spend the rest of my years with her, so I believed it would, could, happen over time.

Well, shortly after we were married, Aunt Mildred died. It was during the winter, and I had contracted a horrendous cold, sore throat, and fever. It was probably the flu. We couldn't make it to the wake on Thursday. I was a mess, but it was Aunt Mildred. On Friday, after Barb finished with teaching, I picked her up, and off we went to Hartford. It's a big hour south and west of Grand Rapids, so we arrived just at the end of the midday showing.

We drove past the mortuary, and Barb said, "You missed it. It's back there on the right."

I explained that she would be further down the street at a friend's place. Sure enough, there had to be fifty cars parked along the main street and side streets. When we went in, the blast of hot air and smell of smoke blew past us and out into the front yard. The foyer, which had a stairs leading to the second story, had folks sitting on the steps, and a hallway leading to the rear was also cogged with folks, but I didn't really recognize anyone. On the left was a large opening into a parlor with another large opening to the right and at the back of the room with pocket doors that were open to accommodate the crowd.

Aunt Mildred was in her casket, more or less propped up in the back corner with a table in front of her with whiskey bottles and glasses at the ready. Through the haze of smoke, I saw my cousin, Doyle, heading toward me, arm extended, pleased by my presence.

"Jaysus, Mary, and Joseph, I'm sorry Mildred is gone. We will all miss her so. She has always been there," I muttered.

Before I knew what hit me, I had about three shots of Jameson in me to see Aunt Mildred off, to clear my throat, and to catch up with everybody else. "You sound terrible, but this will help," Cousin Doyle explained.

It was at this point that I remembered Barb, my wife, the former "schismatic heretic" from a strong Dutch background who had heard of such Catholic traditions and Irish customs. I turned toward the opening off the foyer. Through the smoke, which hung down to about one's waste in heavy clouds, I could just make her out. She was standing in the doorway, searching for me with this expression I will never forget. It was written on her face in large letters. "My relatives were right. They do act like this. It's not made up. It's not fiction. It is not malicious rumor. It is true, every bit of it," her expression seemed to be saying.

The look was not of disgust or condemnation. It was one of amazement. Although her folks smoked, they could not hold a match to the Irish, my Irish and my relatives. She began to squint as I reached her.

I said, "I'm sorry I lost you there for a moment. Come and see Doyle and Marlene and the rest. Everybody we know is in here."

It is odd, but I don't recall seeing my folks or brothers that night. I'm sure they were all there, but the whiskey was taking a toll. I don't know where we spent the night. I suppose we might

Aunt Mildred holding me; her kids, Nancy and Doyle,
in the summer of 1945

have driven back to our apartment in Grand Rapids for the night. Gas was cheap back then.

The funeral mass was solemn. It was a black day for the family, and we shared the loss of the matriarch of the clans. The mantle would now fall on my mother's shoulders. There was universal sadness throughout the family and Hartford since many of the old family friends still lived there or returned for "the passing" of one of theirs.

Doyle asked me to be a pallbearer. In my weakened state, I feared the worse.

I had seen the worst at funerals before. They came back to me now. My brothers and I were often asked to serve Saturday funerals because we were available from the neighborhood. We were willing to give up an hour and a half on Saturday morning because we would make five bucks a piece for our participation. One in particular stuck in my mind. It was in the spring. After the funeral mass, we headed across the street to Resurrection Cemetery for the graveside invocation. Everything was in order. The tent canopy was up for the family. I held the crucifix and was flanked by two of my brothers who held lit candles. The priest had his breviary, a bucket of holy water, and a hand-held holy water sprinkler. We were between the grave with the casket resting on the elevator contraption and the family. The widow was sobbing, her daughter was crying, and a son was very solemn. The priest was saying a few last words when I noticed that my brother on my right was fidgeting about. He was scuffing the artificial grass weave that the cemetery crew spread out in front of the grave to cover up the dirt and mud from the disturbed ground.

As I turned my head slightly while still holding the crucifix, I whispered under my breath, "Knock it off."

Then, I saw him slowly slide down as if on his knees on the artificial grass, which was slowly caving in from his weight. He slid down under the carriage holding the coffin right into the grave. Obviously, the ground was thawing, and the sides of the grave were crumbling. About that time, my other brother followed suit. I took several steps forward and whispered to the priest, "You'd better hurry up or we're all going to be in there."

The family was terribly agitated and became horror stricken when my brothers started yelling for help. One of them threw the candleholder, minus the candle, out of the hole and started to climb out, only to have the rest of the artificial grass give way and nearly bring down the priest and several folding chairs into the hole as well. People were jumping up and knocking chairs over and pushing further toward the back of the tent. This was turning into a circus. I couldn't help but laugh.

I just stepped aside and started to laugh as quietly as I could. My brothers, who had been rescued by the mortuary staff, eventually joined me. We really tried to maintain some decor, reverence, and solemnity, but we couldn't. The more we tried not to laugh, the more we did laugh.

We were trying to hold it in. We shook violently and made muffled noises with our mouths, trying to stifle the deep-down laughs. It seemed it was all the more funny because it was supposed to be so serious.

We were eventually dismissed by the mortuary staff. They were informed that we would never be asked again to serve at a funeral, and we weren't paid to boot. They stuck us in the hearse to muffle our snickering and gasping. We'd have really been pissed if it weren't so damn funny. And all of this filled my memory as I prepared to help at Aunt Mildred's funeral. I prayed, "Sweet Jeysus, please no screw ups. Please. Please. Please."

I was a pallbearer, but was incredibly weak from my bout with the flu or whatever it was that was taking a toll on my health and strength. I feared I was not up to the honor of carrying Aunt Mil into the church, back out to the hearse, then to her final resting place in that cemetery I knew so well from my visits with Mom and Grandma. As we left the church, I felt a wave of nausea sweep over me.

Try to imagine the following as a slow-moving movie. Try to imagine the six of us inhaling the thin, crisp winter air and actually getting lightheaded. What isn't difficult to imagine was that many of us had drained several bottles of Irish whiskey over the past couple of days and, in some cases, the past couple of hours. Try to imagine us starting to slip as we descended the steep steps of the church while trying to steady the coffin with Aunt Mildred inside it.

Good grief, we were sliding down steps, and everything was out of control. This was the worst of all imaginings. Imagine the shrieks. Imagine the horror as the casket took on the life of a huge sled and broke away from us and hit the priest, sending him sprawling at the bottom of the steps. Was I only imagining Aunt Mil spilling out of the sprung coffin lid and peacefully laying in wait there on the sidewalk? The slow motion chaos came to a stop, if not an undignified end there in Hartford, in front of the church. Or did I just imagine it all? I really was quite sick.

The rest was, ah, I do not remember at all. I do not remember going to the cemetery. I do not recall the luncheon afterward, or the ride back to Grand Rapids. It is not a blur. It's a void. I recall nothing. I imagine the rest of the day went all right. I mean, after what I imagined at the church exit, anything might have been all right.

My lovely wife got me home that Saturday night. She tucked me into bed, fortified with non-Irish medicine. I awoke some time on Sunday. I asked her if what I imagined to have happened had really happened. She reassured me by saying, "Everything is okay. All's well that ends well."

I thought, *Now, what the hell does that mean?* I dozed off again, waking finally on Monday. I was embarrassed to ask again about the events on Saturday. Did I screw a thing up? Was I only one of several who caused chaos? Did I only imagine the chaos that seemed real in Hartford? It never came up again. I never asked my mom or Doyle or anyone else. It all was laid to rest with Aunt Mildred.

Maybe I just hallucinated it all. The drink was strong, and it lingered in my weakened state for more than a day. I have come to imagine that I imagined it all. No one ever pointed an accusing finger at me; neither did anyone ever say an unkind word to me about the incident, if it actually happened. But, then again, maybe that was because now my mom was the matriarch, and I was above reproach. I can imagine that. In fact, that seems very likely.

A picture of my children at the time of my youngest son's wedding in 2006. From left to right: Ted, Angie, Amy, Tom, and Cory, Ted's bride.

Chapter Nine

Cars

My brothers and I were raised with cars. Living in Michigan, cars were a given, and they were taken for granted. We pretty much had access to cars anytime we wanted one. At first, my folks only had one auto, but by the time I was in high school, I had access to a car at least one night of the weekend. We ate in the cars, we slept in the cars, we pissed out the windows of the car on the windows of other cars, we drank in the cars, and we mooned out of the cars. We lived in the cars in the '60s.

Sometimes, when we had only one car, there was a line waiting for my dad to come home to see who would get the car. There we were, congregated on the front porch, hoping to be the first to see him coming down Burr Avenue. Usually, he was in a good mood, and we knew by the way he was driving that somebody was going to get the car. He drove a company car that was never more than two years old. It had pick-up; it was usually somewhat stylish, and at less than thirty cents a gallon, it was a crowd pleaser.

Dad had samples of this and that in the trunk that was a permanent feature of his company car. Sometimes, we would get a cardboard box and put all the loose stuff from the trunk in it and hide it in the shelter house at the back of the lot. This could only be accomplished in the dark, so it was a fall and winter maneuver

When this feat could not be accomplished, the stuff in the trunk, at the end of the night, was helter-skelter.

Dad's comments sometimes were directed at the shape of the trunk, but, more often than not, it was directed at the recorded number of miles on the odometer.

Some Saturday mornings, he would come into the house and ask, "Where did you go?" Inevitably, we would answer, "Just around."

He would retort, "You put two hundred miles on the car. Good grief. Where did you go?"

Again, it was always the same answer, whichever one of us was being asked, "I don't know, just around."

"At that rate, you must have gone around the city twenty times," he countered.

When Dad would fly out of Grand Rapids, Mom never let any of us use the car. She was always afraid that we would wreck it, and that she would never hear the end of it. Needless to say, Mom liked being on the delivery end of guilt trips, not the receiving end. Then, about my junior year in high school, the folks

Another photo of some of the Schlosser boys
I had an older brother named John, and I was number two pic-
tured here on the right. Then, there was Joey, Ted, Greg, the
second from the right in this picture, and I suspect this was his
first communion, then Dick and Ronnie who were twins, then
Gary and Frankie. I'm not sure, but I can imagine this could be
the twins by the looks of the matching shirts.

got a second car. It was a good, used, beater that Mom would let
us use almost any weekend night, whether Dad was home or not.
With two autos now, when he was home, two of us could head
out on maneuvers as we called them. Later, in college, they
became "road trips." But, for now, "maneuvers" was the lingo.
Vietnam was just making the news more regularly, and military
lingo was in. "The crew" would ask at school, "Hey, are we going
out on maneuvers tonight?"

"Always," was the standard answer.

We had about a hundred-mile radius from Grand Rapids that
was in striking range. Grand Haven to the west and Newago to
the north had roller-skating rinks which hosted dances in the
winter and spring, after football season. During football season
in the fall, there were always dances in the gym after the games.
We won many more than we lost, so those dances were usually
good events. On homecoming weekend, it was all more formal.

We had as much fun on the informal weekends as the big weekends, and it was cheaper.

Belding and Lowell had dances once in a while, and a time or two, we made it over to Lansing, down to Kalamazoo, and up to Big Rapids. Those really were road trips. But again, the best was usually to be found not far from home. The public schools usually had good dances. The city league schools like Union, Creston, and Ottawa were on the agenda because some of the guys lived in those neighborhoods and knew some of the kids. Living out in the suburbs of Wyoming, Michigan meant Rogers, Godwin, and Kellogsville high schools. During the summer, the only plaza (mall) in the greater Grand Rapids area had dances on the weekends, too.

Also, during the summer, a drive-in theater, just down from Rogers Plaza, had dollar night, a buck for each person in the car, not counting the ones hiding in the trunk. We would get a dollar watermelon, cut a hole in it, fill it with vodka, put it in the freezer for about an hour, and head to the drive-in. It didn't make any difference what was playing; we spent most of the time cruising the back isles, checking cars to see if we could catch a couple "doing it." It was usually just some heavy making out, but that was enough to draw some heavy car rocking and yelling that we caught someone doing the dirty deed. The car usually left for a safer parking spot.

I was particularly fond of this one older-model, second-hand auto Dad got for my mom and for those of us eligible to drive. I took driver's training after my sophomore year in high school. It was no big deal. It wasn't like driving was foreign to me. We'd driven around the neighborhood at night when my folks were gone. I passed it with only one problem.

We had been given this big lecture at the conclusion of the first week about refraining from laughing at students' mistakes while on the driving range, which began the second week. Everything was all right during the first two weeks, but, on Monday of week three, a friend from Saint John's and Catholic Central plowed into a bunch of cones and hit a pole. It was like she had to be taking aim to do this damage. I went into hysterics. I could not stop laughing.

The driving instructor flew out of the car toward me and said, "You are through."

I said, Okay, but you got to admit, that was funny."

I was told to leave the range. I wondered if I was out of the program, but I didn't lose any sleep over it. On the next morning, at nine, I tried to be inconspicuous. The instructor from the day before came up to me and did not tell me to leave; rather, to get into this Dodge with him. He had me drive the range about a half an hour, change a tire, and do parallel and street parking. At the end of two hours, he reluctantly said, "You are a fine driver. You did nothing wrong. Nothing. But you should not laugh at the mistakes of others."

I explained that I knew the girl, Roberta, who crashed yesterday, for a long time, and I was laughing with her.

He said, "We'll see," and he reiterated the rule, "No laughing at other's mistakes."

I agreed, and the rest of that week was a formality for me. I did two more road sessions of about fifteen minutes each before surrendering to some other student who was riding along. On Friday of the third week, I got my conditional driving permit. My folks picked me up at the range, and we headed out for Yellowstone and Jackson Hole. I drove about twenty-five hundred miles in all kinds of conditions and on all kinds of roads over the next three weeks. It was a hell of an experience, and it kept me out of trouble in the backseats of the station wagon. I scared my mother to death on some of the roads out west, along gorges and drop offs. But I was a seasoned driver by the beginning of my junior year.

When I got home, just in time for football practice, I was allowed to drive my mom's car to morning and late-afternoon practice. Once school classes started in the fall, I couldn't drive to school. One day, I came home, and the car was sitting in the driveway, but the rear end was accordioned right up to the rear seat. It had really been tagged. She (Mom) had been in the left-hand lane, ready to make a turn when somebody plowed into the rear of the car. I think she had three of the boys with her.

Apparently, she came out of the car swinging. Bystanders were still restraining her when the police showed up. The driver of the other car's getting a substantial ticket did not alleviate her anger. What added insult to injury was the fact that she was going to the family auto insurance agent when she was hit.

For about two weeks, we had to drive the car with the trunk pushed right up to the backseat. The rear wheels nearly overlapped the rear bumper. I have no idea how the gas tank avoided being ruptured.

Every night, I put a big sign on the rear of the car as it sat in the driveway that said in big, bold letters MOM'S WORK. She didn't see the sign for about a week, but, eventually, someone told her about it. She interrogated us all and, finally, narrowed it down to two of us. I still don't know how, but she settled on me as the culprit, and I paid. I didn't drive it for a month after it was fixed. Each day I was at school, she would hang a sign on the newly fixed car, which read, STILL FIXED, ROG ISN'T DRIVING IT YET. Revenge was sweet to her, and she relished in embarrassing her sons.

My dad's car was not immune from disaster either. My folks went out east to a conference at some big resort in New York State. At the conference, the guys "worked" in the morning and screwed around in the afternoon while the wives had the whole day at leisure. A district manager from here in Grand Rapids drove my folks and his wife out there. Incomprehensibly, my folks left us all home alone without a chaperone. I have no idea what they were thinking or what drug they were testing for the company.

The very first thing my brother, Greg, did was take my dad's company car out to some field party and run over a stump, ripping the oil pan, the transmission, and gas tank off the car. I have no idea how he got home; for that matter, I have no idea why he even came home. He was dead. But lady luck was smiling on him that weekend. All of his buddies turned in the beer cans and took up a collection to fix the car. A neighbor family ran a junkyard and fixed him up with a mechanic. By Saturday night, the damage was fixed. It ran over the money he had, but he made some arrangement to pay it off with both the junkyard family and this mechanic. I thought, *The luck of the Irish.*

My brother, Greg, was the only one of us who didn't look at all like the rest of us. We all looked Irish with our dark hair and dark eyes. Greg was a blue-eyed blond. The Borden Dairy milk deliverer was also a blue-eyed blond, so Mom and Greg got kidded a lot about it. Everybody got a laugh about it, especially as we boys got older and understood the naughty innuendo. Well, everyone but my dad thought it was funny. To start a row, one of us would get their girlfriend to pen a note, and we would leave it on dad's desk in the basement saying that "JB" had paid a visit lasting about half an hour while Dad was out of town. The neighbors were concerned about a scandal. Nothing was done in front of us boys but there were muffled "discussions" that went on behind closed bedroom doors. It was great.

I don't recall Dick ever doing anything to my folk's autos, but he did some real outrageous deeds with his own car. He had a Duster that had about two hundred thousand miles on it before the odometer was unhooked. He had some problems with the law over a number of issues that resulted in his driver's license being confiscated. Not deterred, he kept driving the "Dust Mop." The cops finally got wise, so they thought, and they took the license plate off the Duster. It sat for about a month in the folks' side yard, near the garage.

One evening, my wife and I went out to visit the folks, and Dick cornered me and said, "Will you drive me up to such and such grocery store?"

I said, "Yeah." Turning to my wife, I said, "Barb, I'll be right back. Dick needs a lift to the store." Off we went.

As we pulled into the parking lot and I headed for the store door, Dick said, "Slow down and let me out by this row of cars. Pick me up on the row over there."

I, as a little slow, thinking that maybe he spotted a couple of bucks on the ground or a couple of returnable beer or pop cans, and he was going to collect them before heading into the store for cigarettes or something.

By the time I rounded the end of the cars in that isle he was waiting for me about halfway down. "Aren't you going in," I asked. He just smiled as he revealed a license plate he had taken off some car back there. I asked him if he was insane. He said he was sick of walking and mooching rides everywhere. He drove for about a month before he was caught and detained for several months.

After this bout with insanity, I thought he was on the straight and narrow when I got a call one night with the following story. He had gone to an outdoor concert or rodeo to the north of the city. He knew he had a gas leak in the "Dust Mop's" gas tank but thought it would be of no consequence out in a field—a dry field, a *very dry* field. All was well until he returned to the car to fetch a packet of cigarettes. He lit up and walked down about four rows when his cigarette went out. Lighting it back up, he threw the match on the ground. Well, on the grass, to be more precise. It started a little fire that he stomped out. Or so he thought.

He was about ten steps away when he heard a "whoosh." All the cars on the end of the rows caught on fire. He knew immediately what had happened. He kept on moving and made it into the crown before all hell broke loose. He ditched his shirt and acted amazed at the damage. He figured he'd get another car out of this unsolved mysterious fire. Unfortunately, the fire investigators traced the fire to his Duster. He got out of serious criminal charges because they couldn't prove he knew he had a leaking gas tank. But three or four auto insurance companies were after him in civil proceedings. Being legally destitute, I think, he beat those raps, too; again, the luck of the Irish.

I might casually mention that one Christmas, my brother, Dick, piled all of his old toys in the corner of the bedroom he shared with two others and lit them on fire. Fortunately, my folks walked in on time to douse the fire. Dick had this thing with fire, and, way back then, he was saved by the luck of the Irish.

Another brother, Gary, had a bad habit of losing Dad's car. He would go out and get buzzed up and forget where he parked it. Someone would get him home, but, come morning, there was no car. He had no idea of where to look. The folks would go nuts. He would start checking around, and, eventually, through the help of friends, he would locate it and retrieve it. I don't recall him ever destroying a car like some of the others, but he could be on the "shit list" with the rest of us. Dad would get as upset with us for spilling a glass of milk as he did when we destroyed a car. We never figured out Dad.

Again, it was Mom who usually enforced any punitive action. One time, Gary lost the car, and Mom had him by the shirtfront pinned up against the front vestibule wall and was demanding to know where he left the car. He said she was so angry that she lifted him off the floor. Now, he was in his junior or senior year in high school, and he was not a dainty young lad. He explained that after a goodnights' sleep, he would be right on it. She was not impressed, and she was in a foul mood and clearly had homicide in mind. Everyone expected her to kill him, but, through some intervention, he made it until dawn, started calling around and located the car on the northwest side of Grand Rapids, a couple of blocks from my brother's, Greg's, apartment—luck of the Irish.

My brother's, Gary's, family at my son's, Ted's, wedding;
my folks are seated with Kathyrn, my brother's daughter.
Standing to the left is Adam, and to the far right is
Andrew, with Gary second from the right.

Luck ran out for me just before I was off to college. A couple of friends of mine got some beer, and we went out toward Lamont, a small picturesque village to the west of Grand Rapids, along the Grand River. The oil light had been showing up for weeks, off and on, and with a few beers under our belts, we decided to ignore the warning one more time.

First, there was the damnedest smoke trailing out the rear of that old Plymouth; then came some shuddering from under the hood. There was no perceived loud noise coming from the engine, although the radio blasting music could have veiled it. But then, there was a rather loud blast, and the car coughed a loud puff of black smoke and died. We opened the hood and checked it out, but none of us were into working on cars; we just drove them. We walked about a mile back to a service station and, finally, bought some oil. What is that old maxim, "too little too late?" We called one of the fella's parents. His dad came out and picked us up.

I was waiting on the porch for my dad when he came in. I explained the condition of the car, leaving out several unnecessary parts of the story, concentrating on the critical and essential points concerning the car. That night, we went out to Lamont and hauled the car back to the house.

The only thing he said was, "When the oil light goes on, there is a reason for it. Stop and check the oil level. You got it?"

Oh yeah, I got it. I had no car for about a month. But that was the end of it. No more comments from Dad, and Mom never said a word. Dad was out of town by air on the next Monday, so Mom had his car, and the rest of us were out of luck because of my foolishness.

I learned a valuable lesson in that episode. Let your friends drive if the oil light is showing. There is only so much money to go around, and, if you intend to buy beer, it's better that their auto report any low oil level than your folks' or your auto. What baffled me was that Mom never said a thing, probably because her necessity for an auto was not hindered by this mistake. When Dad got back weeks later, they got another beater, and I was off to college, and my brothers picked up where I left off.

I don't remember exactly how many cars we went through between the time the oldest of us started driving and the last boy left home. It had to be about fifteen, at least. There was never a trade-in car; each of them was rendered useless at the end. We took no prisoners. The car we did in was junk.

Chapter Ten

Catholic School

When in grade school, one year blended into another. You moved from one room to another. A kid or two wouldn't return at the start of the New Year, but a few new faces would join the class, too. High school was different. There were definite changes from year to year—moving up to the varsity and driving cars for example. One of the best weekend nights always took place at one of the Polish Halls. Now, you had to dress up somewhat because we were the original wedding crashers. Oh yeah. We'd show up at the reception and say, "Bride's side," or "Groom's side," and say one of the guys still coming had the gift. By the time the master and mistress of ceremony knew what was happening, we were changing our shirts in the "john," and locating the open bar and food table. One night, I danced with the bride for about three dances before her husband of three hours finally cut in. I explained in as sober a voice as I could muster that his bride "reminded me so much of my sister who had recently gotten married, and I missed her so." This dumb ass believed me, and I got another two or three dances with the bride who was well-built and showing some of it in her bridal gown. I thought my friends would go nuts.

There were two Catholic girls' schools in Grand Rapids at that time, and around Halloween and Valentine's Day, they had dances. They charged a buck or two for one to get in, and one usually had the pick of the litter. There was a one-to-ten ratio of "lookers" to "bow wows." The sisters patrolled the dance floor, and, if you got too "intimate," they were on you like a rabid dog. As all Catholics know, nuns are cloistered, and "sisters" are not (but many of us thought some of them should have been). Two warning were followed up by being tossed out. It was like a two-strike rule. Inevitably, a row would start over a refund from whoever couldn't stay at the dance. It seemed that these sisters were always older than Methuselah, and you could argue with them indefinitely, and they would stand there and continue to argue their point. They were used to girls, but we could "josh em" for hours. Even some of the girls caught on and had a good laugh about it.

We would try to hook up with the girls after the dance, but, between the chaperones and fastidious parents, we got nowhere. We would head for Monroe Avenue and drive the circuit and end up getting in a fight. We lived for the weekends.

I would see the guys sparingly during the summertime because most of us worked, and I spent time at my parents' cottage about twenty miles north of Grand Rapids. In August, we would start to gather at parks on the west side of Grand Rapids to get serious about football. We would run some, do calisthenics, and play tag to get in shape. Most of us lifted weights on our own. Schools, at least Catholic Central, didn't have weight rooms at this time. There were only so many sports as well. Football and cross-country in the fall, swimming and basketball during the winter, and track, baseball, and maybe golf and tennis, I don't remember for sure about these last two.

With fall ball came school, and, quite frankly, I enjoyed being in certain classes. My mom went to Catholic Central starting her freshman year, but my dad didn't start until his junior year. But my brothers and I had some of the Dominican Sisters at Catholic that our folks had way back when. Several of the good sisters had had my dad. The Dominicans were supposed to be "different" from the other orders that staffed the Catholic grade schools for the most part. In grade school at Saint John's, we had a different order, and I can't say I remember too much good about them;

neither did they leave a positive impression on me, except that I was "positive." I didn't care for them. It was probably my youth. But you see, I knew quite a bit about history and geography, and this sister I had in the sixth or seventh grade made a mistake in one or the other subjects. I corrected her, and she insisted that she was correct.

I was a jerk and corrected her again in a boisterous fashion that was an affront to her exalted position and dignity. She had jerked me around all year, and this was my time to shine. She reprimanded me by making me stay after school and having me write fifty times, "When I am corrected, I will quietly accept the correction and any punishment for being rude, boisterous, and disruptive." Instead, I wrote, "When I am right, I will defend my position no matter what." She had left the room as I finished my draft, so I put it on her desk and went home.

My senior graduation picture, 1963

I explained the circumstances to my mom and defended my actions. She simply said, "We'll see." The next day, all hell broke loose. I had to go to the office at the start of school. I sat there for about an hour, and, ultimately, I was taken to Sister

"Dachau's" office who was the principal while she called my mother (we had names for all the "good" sisters like this one: Sister Treblinka, Sister Auschwitz, Sister Buchenwald, etc.). There was a lengthy exchange, and I was sure happy I had clued my mom in on the situation. I was eventually asked to wait in the outer office. About ten minutes later, I was told to report to my classroom. No one said another thing at school.

At lunch, my mom put everything in perspective, and in language I clearly understood. "You were right," Mom said, "but you blew it by embarrassing her and embarrassing me. You were right and wrong at the same time. Don't do it again. You got it?"

I said, "Yeah."

"Don't be an ass and blow your point. Think," she said, concluding the discussion.

I had a couple of other encounters with the good sisters at Saint John's, and I looked forward to a new school and a new religious order in high school. During my freshman year, I had an old sister for Freshman English who died during the Christmas break. There were a couple of us in the class who were goofing around, and there were more than five hundred and fifty freshman, so she probably taught five or six sections and had a couple of clowns per class. It couldn't have been easy for the old girl, and none of the horseplay was personal or directed toward her. We were just immature jerks. But she died; there was no denying that, and we certainly didn't delay her fate and, quite possibly, hastened her demise.

On our return to classes in January to complete the first semester, the principal of the East Building, which housed freshman and sophomores, an old battle-ax Dominican that my dad had back in the '30s, Sister Irene, came into our classroom and said, "Congratulations, you killed sister so and so. You will get a new teacher who isn't going to take any guff. Three of you will be placed in other class sections." I ended up in her class, which was double jeopardy as far as I was concerned.

We had done grammar the first semester and were scheduled to do literature the second half. In the new class, they had done literature the first semester and were scheduled to do grammar the second half. I got a full year of grammar with Sister Irene, one of Dad's old buddies as it turned out; we diagrammed sentences and identified participles, gerunds, and the rest. I thought I was going to die. Sister Irene had a habit of resting her elbow on her desk and cradling her chin in her fisted hand, but she kept her index finger straightened out along the side of her face so she could quick draw it like a gun and point it at you like a gun. She kind of cocked her mouth and squinted her right eye like she was taking aim at you. I was in her sights the rest of my freshman year. By Easter, she was complimenting me on both class work and homework. My grade in English improved considerably, but my dislike for English, the English, anything English was growing exponentially with each day. My folks found it refreshingly humorous for different reasons.

The best part of my sophomore year was not doing grammar in English class. The second best thing was we went undefeated in football that fall. For homeroom, I had a Latin teacher named Sister Rose. She was notorious for being a stickler on Latin Grammar, and I thought, *Shitibus, here we go again; only this time, it is going to be in a foreign language.* But when I looked on my class schedule, I was to go to another room with another instructor. My Latin teacher was only interested in translating and Caesar's Gaulic Wars was straightforward and interesting. From there, we went into mythology, epigrams, and poetry. I liked Sophomore Latin.

When our Latin instructor was absent (She had to be ninety years old and was sick quite a bit. The luck of the Irish, amen.), we just translated for the substitute teacher, who more often than not was not a Latin instructor at all. We would write out the translations and hand them in. If I got done early, I would get a "pass" to go to Sister Rose's class to ask her a Latin question. There was a cloakroom with both ends open up at the front of the room between two doors that led to the hallway. I would quietly go in and hide among the jackets and coats for a bit in case Sister Rose heard the door open. When I was sure it was safe to be mischievous, I would switch gloves, scarves, hats—anything to cause a row at dismissal. Sometimes, I would place notes supposedly written by some student under someone's coat like it fell out of their pocket. It would contain some BS, again to start a squabble.

Sophomore year was decidedly better than freshman year. I didn't get in any fights with classmates, whereas, during freshman year, I had a couple of significant fights, one with another freshman over a jammed locker, and another after a dance with a senior who was an ass. That one was a draw, but he was older, bigger, and actually got the worse of it, so I was establishing my name. My dad was disgusted when he learned of the fights, but my mom was proud of me.

Junior year was a mixed bag. I have already spoken of my chemistry fiasco. After starting a couple of football games, I sustained a blown-out knee. I was physically and psychologically shot. I stayed on the team but kept getting hurt, and it was dawning on me that my football days were numbered. That realization was difficult. I planned on college ball, and my plans were no longer realistic. The harder I played, the more difficult it became, and the greater the injuries became. It was over, but I couldn't let it go. I wasn't sure there was life after ball. I was stupid.

Actually, it wasn't all bad that third year of high school. I met some guys then who have stayed as my friends these forty odd years now. These guys, along with my older friends, remained the greatest gifts of my high school years. Several of these guys were Grand Rapids west-siders whom I had gone to kindergarten with, and it was like a reunion. These boys were nuts, and they came to Catholic Central with new ideas of mayhem and sedition. There was only one Catholic High School for both sexes in the city and surrounding areas at that time. If you were from the west side of the Grand River, which split Grand Rapids, you took the first two years of high school at a west side high school that only catered the freshman and sophomore years, then you crossed the river, and came to Catholic Central. If you played sports, you could come straight to Catholic Central in your freshman and sophomore years. We went to school with guys from all over the city and suburbs. We met them from different parishes in both our freshman and junior years.

We had twenty minutes for lunch, and there was no "hot lunch" or "cafeteria food," so we "brown-bagged" it. There were a half a dozen canteen machines that sold snack food, chips, and twenty-cent pies. Eight or ten of us would buy cherry pies and wait until everyone was seated and eating. At a quiet countdown, we would fling the pies over our shoulders, and they would sail about three tables in the back of us. The "cool guys" sat at that table, mimicking the Chad Mitchell Trio, wearing their blue and white striped shirts. All of a sudden "whack," "splat," and the word "shit" would erupt from them.

We would turn around in a show of disgust and say, "Oh no. What a shame."

The lunchroom coordinator would come out of the faculty lunchroom to investigate the ruckus. Finding no evidence of guilt, only evidence of pie stain, he would announce that the whole lunch period would report after school to the cafeteria for a penalty.

Everyone suspected, but no one saw the origin of the bombardment or actually saw the pies being slung. After a night or two of staying an hour after school, innocent students' parents would complain, and the penalty hour would cease. In a week or two, we'd do it again, and the same routine would happen. It was the blue and white stripes that brought out the cherry pie in us. We thought it would be patriotic with the red, white, and blue. The "cool guys" stopped wearing their blue and white striped shirts, and the pie flinging abruptly stopped as well.

On our senior year, a kid who transferred in from the seminary was simply outstanding. The boy's name was Willard. I've only known a couple of Willards, but high school Willard was in a league all his own. He took to tormenting the gold fish that this one biology sister was raising in a huge tank in the front of the room. Willard was small, so he sat in the front of the room. In Catholic schools, the practice was to seat you alphabetically and/or by height.

Willard would flick this flavored dissolvable candy into the fish tank. Cherry red, orange, plum purple, blueberry blue, on it went until the fish would swim around whipped into a frenzy. The water splashed out of the tank; the turbulence was so great that the front row of students would get wet. Willard had the front row bring towels and goggles one day. The old sister was not amused. She sent for the assistant principal who kept us after school for a couple of days.

The next week, he threw about a dozen Fizzies and a handful of alkaselsors into the tank, and the fish started to get violent. The turbulence was exceptional. The waves were splashing out on the floor, over desks, soaking front-row students. There was pandemonium. Then, the fish started leaping out—first, a small one, then a big one, and, finally, the granddaddy of them all flopped onto the floor. Willard started talking about the fishes and the loaves, but the good sister failed to get the point. Willard accused her of letting God's creatures die unnecessarily. That was it. When the assistant principal came this time, we were to stay after school until he got sick of us. After two and a half weeks, some friends started painting the priest's car that was parked in the lot off a rough street, Division Avenue. He couldn't prove any of us were involved, but he told us no more penalty hall.

The entire faculty stood in the hallways during the exchange of classes to make sure nothing inappropriate happened. I had a friend in a physics class who simply watched the biggest-boobed girl in our senior class come into the class, walk across the front of the room as the bell rang, and sit down. The old sister casually walked over to Dave, picked him up in his desk, (I mean she lifted him while he was sitting in his desk), and slugged him with her fist.

He grabbed his face and said, "What did you do that for, sister? I didn't do anything."

She simply retorted, "I knew what you were thinking."

So, anything went in or between classes as far as the faculty was concerned, and they were on the lookout for any action, word, or thought that violated the code. Life was brutal in parochial school.

Willard discovered that if you hurled a penny up into the Styrofoam ceiling, it stuck there for five minutes, give or take a few seconds. He got everyone in this science class to heave a penny up into the ceiling just moments before the sister returned from her hallway duty. Sister came into class and started the prayer as the pennies started dropping from the ceiling. Willard led us in a stirring rendition of "Pennies from Heaven." We were into the third repeat when the assistant principal, Father M., showed up again.

He was pissed. "You are the worst class in the history of this school. But there are only about ten percent of you who are rotten. But you disgrace the rest of the class. You should be ashamed."

Sure, right, we all knew that the rest of them would like to have been like us, but we wouldn't let them in to our gang, which became known as the "Ten Per Centers."

Years later, I was asked to do a reading at a mass prior to a "Class Reunion of the CC Class of 1963." Guess who was saying the mass? Good old Father M., the assistant principal. I made sure to introduce myself as "Rog Schlosser, I am a Ten Per Center" before I read from the Gospel. Father M. did not appreciate the little jab.

The best and most memorable occurrence happened in the spring of 1963, just before graduation. The emptied fish tank was now being used by the good sister as a frog habitat. She was raising the frogs to be dissected in her biology classes, thus, saving the school on the cost of purchasing them from some supplier. One day, Willard stood by the door behind the sister doing hall duty, and he collected everyone's ink pen filler. We all had ink pens that unscrewed, allowing the ink filler and a spring to be retrieved. He collected the long cylindrical ink fillers.

He said, "Get rid of the rest of the ink pens."

Everyone got into his seat and waited for the fireworks. We had no idea of what he had planned, but, with only a week to go, it had to be memorable.

Class started with a prayer, no pennies dropped this time, and everything seemed in order. Sister walked around the room, taking roll. Then, she started to quiz us about yesterday's class and last night's textbook reading. Everything was going fine until she turned to go down the center row. She let out a shriek that had to be heard by people five miles away. She had collapsed in a vacant chair at the rear of the room next to the frog-breeding tank. One hand was still clutching a side of the tank when the whole class surrounded her to see what was wrong.

It was then that we saw what elicited her horrible scream. The frogs in the tank had all been pierced by the ink fillers and were positioned in the tank as if they had been attacked by Indians. Willard had arranged them propped up against a wall of the tank or against a rock with an ink filler or two sticking in them. Some were draped over rocks, little logs and feeding containers with ink cartridge "arrows" protruding from them. Some had their front arms and webbed paws clutching the "arrows" while others were impaled to cardboard food containers. It was right out of MGM. A laughing roar that had to be heard ten miles away now replaced sister's shriek.

We didn't have long to wait for all hell to break loose. It was like an inquisition this time. Willard kept whispering that Father M.'s middle name was Torquamada. Willard and I had to be the only two guys in the class who knew the reference, but everyone sensed it was associated with persecution. We weren't going to graduate; we couldn't go through the graduation line; we were going to have to pay for the dead frogs; we would have to work at the school for a month during the summer. This last rumor brought a smile to a couple of our faces. "Were they nuts? Can you imagine what we could do here in a month? Not having to be bothered by classes?" They came to see the folly of it all, and, after a collection was taken up to replace the frogs, all was dropped if not forgotten. It was the last great classroom prank delivered by the "Class of '63," well, some of the class anyway, the "Ten Per Centers."

The very last thing I will relate involved the Ten Per Centers as a group venture that happened every day. At 11:15 every morning, Monday through Friday, mass was held in the cathedral of Saint Andrews that was situated right next to Catholic Central. The whole senior class went every day. From day one, "TR" picked the lock to the church basement and the Ten Per Centers went underground. We never attended daily mass, not once our senior year. Now, the cathedral basement had a pool table, a TV, and nice lounging furniture for church clubs and organizations. All of these facilities got good use and were greatly appreciated by the boys. We could hear the shuffle of feet for communion and, about five minutes later, more shuffling as the students came out of church. We would emerge from the basement and join our classmates heading for the cafeteria.

As you can see from this narration, cafeteria was not necessarily the best period of the day, but it was close. We always had a few guys in every class who were Ten Per Centers, even though some pulled out and went to public school after a year or two. I usually told my mom what went on at school a month or two after the event, when the dust settled. In some cases, she put on that she was horrified; in others, she really laughed. But she always appreciated my telling her the stories.

Years later, when I would run into one or another of the old gang, news concerning this one or that one cheered us up or brought on a serious pause. We stayed close for years, and although the formal get-togethers have become fewer than in the past, we still meet once in a while and run into one another constantly. Inevitably, it comes up, "God, do you remember the time....?" And we always do. But, unlike the football games that we win more of now and by greater spreads, the Ten Per Center's stories never have to be inflated. They can and do stand on their own.

In spite of these stories, my beautiful wife insisted on our kids going to Catholic schools. In the second grade, my oldest daughter made her first confession. This would be her second sacrament, and this would be a significant step for her. I didn't work on Thursdays, so I was her school-room "mother," along with some real mothers of her classmates. After the confession ritual over in the church, we "mothers" put on a party back in school for the recipients of conditional forgiveness.

The officiating priest was a special guest to our classroom party celebration.

The priest was charismatic, and a charlatan in my book. By way of explanation, let me illustrate by completing the story. He posed as a "seer" of sorts. Well, I wore a sports jacket to school that day, and I was standing off to the side in the room, allowing the real mothers to fuss over the party when the priest came over and stood next to me.

I nodded politely, and he responded by asking, "Are you a police officer?"

I stared at him in confusion and asked, "What?" That was the last question I expected from the priest.

He repeated, "Are you a police officer?"

I immediately remembered that one of my daughter's classmates had a father, also named "Roger," who was a police officer. He had obviously asked one of the women what my name was and, upon hearing the name "Roger," jumped to the conclusion that I was the cop. Then, to advance his reputation that he was specially blessed as a mentalist, he had asked me his question.

I answered him, "Does it show?"

He smiled, quite content with his predicting powers and said confidently, "I thought so!"

I smiled and thought to myself, *You charlatan.* After I left the school, I drove home with the thought that on the day of my daughter's first reconciliation, I purposely deceived her confessor. What a day for both of us.

Years later, I told my wife and my kids this story, and we all got a good laugh out of it. Where else but in Catholic schools could such an ironic twist of events take place? The other three kids also went to Catholic schools, and now, my grandchildren go there. It's a special place that is full of possibilities of education on several levels. These Catholic schools are simply the best for a lot of reasons, not the least of which is that my wife has taught at West Catholic High School here in Grand Rapids for years.

Most, if not all, of my friends had trouble at one time or another with the clergy and lay teachers at school. The teachers were overall pretty decent people. There are always exceptions and a couple in particular are worth mentioning. The principal at Catholic Central was so pissed at me that he wanted to box me. I had reconstructive knee surgery shortly after my boxing stint in the Golden Gloves during my senior year. I had to go around on crutches for weeks. My doctor's office was about half a mile from school, so I scheduled an appointment just at the end of school. My last hour of school was a study hall. I went to the office to ask if I might miss my last hour, study hall, and the closing homeroom at the end of the school day since I would be heading to the doctor. The secretaries in the school office said, "Okay." But the principal, Father Y., came out of his office and asked what was going on.

After my request and explanation, he told me to step into his office for a moment. Once inside, he said I was one of the biggest disappointments he ever knew, academically and athletically. I could leave early for the doctor's appointment, he said. "I don't care where you go. I don't care if you never come back. If you do, I'd like to schedule a little boxing match over in the gym sometime to show you a thing or two."

He had been a chaplain in the army and was still with the National Guard. So, he was a "bad ass," and wanted to impress me I guess. I thought, *What an ass.* I just walked out of his office and headed for the appointment.

Another of my fond memories involved a second priest at the high school. It occurred about the same time as the previous confrontation. During after-school penalty hall, that lasted approximately one hour (15:30 to 16:30), Father M. would make me get out of my desk, gather up my crutches, and hobble about three steps to hand him the sign-in sheet for the penalty hall. He would not make the effort to save me the trouble of having to get up and hobble back to turn in the sheet. I was incensed one night, and I flipped the sign-in sheet on his desk and headed off on my crutches for the elevator that I was allowed to use. He left the penalty hall and caught up with me at the elevator. On the way down to the ground floor, he stopped the elevator, saying, "I know you are upset for what I did, but I have to act this way to establish my authority and reputation."

Then, he proceeded to berate me for planning to attend a state college instead of the local Catholic college. He said such an action would be a "sin." I laughed and thought of my mom who I have no doubt knew as much Catholic doctrine and spoke with as much "authority" as this priest.

I said, "You wouldn't know a sin if it bit you in the ass."

He backed off the elevator, and I proceeded to leave the school to wait for my ride home. In spite of encounters like this, I never had any of the problems that surfaced later about priests and young boys and girls.

During the height of the clerical scandals over pedophilia, a couple of the guys and I questioned each other, "You ever had a bad encounter with a priest? You know, a pedophile."

The answer was always "no," or a resounding "never."

So, for all their faults, and they had their faults, they were what I would call normal faults, not kinky faults. Maybe we were just lucky back then. I knew good priests and bad ones, good sisters and bad ones. There were good lay teachers and bad ones. My friends had what I would call good parents, and there were some who I thought were bad ones.

The religious were no different than any of our parents. But old Father P. from Saint John Vianney had enlightened me and put it in perspective for me when he said, "We priests are human. We are 98 percent human. The 2 percent that's sacred is our index finger and our thumb, which holds the Sacred Host."

If the truth were known, old Father P., who had sincere talks with me when I walked him home from our house at night, was not only sincerely honest but also an anticlerical priest. He reiterated that the best thing the Catholic Church was doing locally and in the United States was in education. He warned to cut through the "BS;" "but take the math and Latin. "It will serve you well," he said. His prediction was correct and learning how to read, write, do math, and follow directions gets you a long way in college, work, and the real world. Those parochial teachers had personal issues, but they projected a program based on and for success. They bought into a two thousand-year-old ideal that transcended the institution of the Church. Father P. taught me to differentiate between the people and the tradition, and to respect the tradition and what it stood for, in spite of the people. That was an essential lesson. I think he was right.

But my mom was the supreme anticleric. There were only two priests whom she genuinely admired and respected, other than the Pope. The rest were just "jokers" and "wanna bees," trying to be what they never would be. "They are reverend fathers, only because they wear the collar," she used to say.

My brothers and I never questioned Mom's judgment. She had gone through Catholic schools and understood the truth, the good, and the beautiful from the rest of it. She knew the way, the truth, and life, and she taught her sons by supplementing the schools. Furthermore, she'd say, "See and make humor in your life." After all, she was somehow related to you know who's mother and spoke with authority. Amen.

If it appears that I have ended this story on a too serious a note, let me explain. Although I have ignored the academic contribution the parochial schools provided me with, be assured they did contribute to my intellectual well-being. They introduced me to a wealth of information, the content of which I have added to over the years through both formal and informal study, just as college and university were augmented by extensive travel and personal contacts. Although the formal study of taking college classes ended many years ago, the informal study has continued on many levels, leading me to every continent but Antarctica (which I have no desire to visit).

I do believe that my parents afforded me the support to take advantage of opportunities provided by the several educational institutions I attended. Saint John Vianney Grade School and Catholic Central High School prepared me for Grand Rapids Junior College and Western Michigan University, which, in turn, made a sabbatical at the University of Notre Dame possible. Catholic schools, as I said previously, are the best. They certainly were for me anyway. The content was there, even if slanted and questionable, and the rigors of content and style brought out the desire in me to learn more and teach. I owe much to all the institutions of learning which accepted the challenge of teaching me.

Having said this, I am and will always be indebted to the Catholic schools. They shaped me even when I fought it. I am what I am and who I am because of the Catholic schools. I am thankful that my children have all gone there, that my grandchildren are currently schooled there, and that my wife is a part of it now, too. To have been a part of this program was to have been initiated into a sorority and fraternity like no other. It was like a baptism that lasted for years, the formative years. We all have experienced the formation of ourselves, just as our ancestors contributed to the physical formation of our bodies. They taught me answers to the "what" of life. Although I have abandoned some of that content, I have retained the "how" to approach life. Catholic schools are an international association that not only suggests the "what ifs" of life, but guides the "what should I be about" in life.

No doubt, the public schools and other parochial schools can attest to educational excellence also. But the Catholic schools are different. The experiences are similar to all educational institutions. But, I say again, the Catholic schools were and remain different.

But, as of late, the most rewarding ongoing education has been my association with the Grand Rapids Community College (GRCC) "Irish Foreign Studies Program." This Irish Program brings students and faculty to Ireland every June. After a rigorous month of formal study here at GRCC, participants travel to Ireland and meet people who are making a new Ireland, who have participated in this process, and who have observed and studied recent developments in Ireland, both the twenty-six counties in the "south" and the six counties in the "north."

Ireland has proven to be such a unique microcosm of an emerging nation and an old historical nation. Her people embody all the complexities that a society can hand out. She is broad in every aspect, yet small enough to get around in. She is narrow on some points and yet broad-minded at the same time. The more I travel there, the more my students discover what I have passed over. They help introduce Ireland to me every year. My Irish friends and acquaintances extend themselves to me like I was family, maybe better now that my mom is gone.

I will close this last chapter with words of wisdom that my mother never directly said, but that she implied time and again. They have become my motto, and my students, colleagues, friends, and others have heard them expressed by me, "Life is too serious to be taken seriously."

Afterward

No one missed us at mass on our senior year. We were the row-dies, and no one missed us. If anyone should have been missed, it should have been us. If anyone needed religion, it was surely the Ten Per Centers. But we were not missed. The mere fact that mass went on day after day without any interruptions should have raised suspicions that something was wrong. Where were they? Where were the troublemakers? Where were the Ten Per Centers? But we were not missed. This turned out to be a valuable lesson: we were expendable, we were not missed, and we were forgotten, except to ourselves. I have cherished these stories right along with my family's stories. My brothers all had stories about school. They told stories about their friends at school. And, like us, they, too, were forgotten as soon as possible.

I'm neither bitter nor am I disappointed. The Catholic schools became legendary institutions because of discipline, order, and academics for sure. But they also were special because of the friends and friendship to be found there and the shared experi-ences. In my case, many of the guys from school were like family then and now, especially since I started losing brothers to a wide assortment of problems, especially heart disease.

My wife has heard most of these tales and has met most of the heroes of these stories. Sometimes, I will be driving along or we will be walking along or we'll be in church, and I start laughing.

She will say, "What are you laughing about?"

I just tell her, "Oh, I was just thinking of something," or "I just remembered something."

She's come to know me and my imagination. I do spend a lot of time in my own little world with my brothers and friends. We are all still young, vibrant, and bad as hell. I won't have it any other way. As I stated at the beginning of this work, the stories are the products of experiences, remembrances, and creative imagination.

I've heard it said by some, "The truth is too painful." Not to remember experiences, not to share experiences, and not to build on those happenings is to cease to be human. The truth is, not to be human, at least once in a while, is painful. We only get so many opportunities to be human. I'll neither be a great hero in the historic sense nor a great academic, philosopher, poet, or writer; hell, I'm not convinced I was a particularly good son, good husband, father, or grandfather. But I've been in the company of some of the most remarkable people in the world. Maybe they, too, are little known to the general public, but they populate my world; they never die, and they always fascinate me, make me laugh, and tickle my imagination. I really like them all, my family and friends. I am better off and just plain better for having had them in my life.

As I write this memoir, I have buried seven brothers and several friends from high school. I miss them all, and they were never expendable; they are missed beyond words, and they will never be forgotten. I had the best of all worlds, brothers by blood and brothers by choice. I remember the stories and what brings them to life are all the guys who have joined my walk through life and have made me laugh for years. What started with my parents' family was extended to a larger family via the parochial schools, and now is kept alive by my family: my wife, my daughters and their husbands, my sons and their wives, my grandchildren, my remaining brother, Gary, his kids, and all the other nephews and nieces. I have laughed more than I have been driven to tears. As I have said more than once throughout this work in one way or another, ignorance is bliss, and being stupid wasn't all that bad. After all, we are all just stupid humans.

It's no mistake that the words "human" and "humor" have the same root. They are connected and overlap. Too many people take themselves seriously. Life is too serious to be taken too seriously. It's just that simple, and you don't have to be a wizard to figure that out. As my mother used to say, "You just have to wake up and die right."

Glossary

My mother had an extensive number of words and phrases that she used in conjunction with everyday language. I have come to understand that many of these words and phrases are common among the Irish. Some are found amid her quotes I cited above. Here is a more thorough listing of her everyday lingo that I find myself using. I have an Irish friend, Dorothy, originally from Chicago, who constantly told me her mother used many of the same phrases. After Dorothy would hear me use one of Mom's phrases, she would smile and nod her head as if agreeing and say, "My mother used to say the same thing."

If these tidbits are universal, I hope they bring a smile to those who are familiar with them. If they are regional, then I hope these items will bring both pleasure and enlightenment to the newly initiated. In both cases, enjoy them if you can.

I will list them in no particular order as my Irish mother would want, except that those relating to the divine family will come first.

* * * * * * * * * * * *

"What in God's name....?" — Obviously, "What are you doing, thinking?"

"What in God's Holy name....?" — Damningly, the same as above, "What are you doing/thinking?"

"Jesus, Mary, and Joseph...." — Astonishment at something done or said

"Jeysus." — Same as above, "What are you doing/thinking/saying?"

"Sweet Jeysus." — Same as above, but with added astonishment

"My God...." — Same as above, but with disgust

"What/Who in Sam Hill...?" — A prefatory statement causing us to pause and reflect; still do not know who Sam Hill is or was

"I'll trade you off for a horse and shoot the horse...." — You are expendable.

"There will be two hits: when I hit you and you hit the floor." — You are going down.

""I'll knock you into the middle of next week." — Same as above, but with consciousness returning in a week

"You won't know if you're foot or horseback." — Like above, you are going down.

"You're going to make it by the skin of your teeth." — You just are going to be on time.

"I'll beat you to within an inch of your life." — A mathematical distance between life and death

"Who put a nickel in you?" — You are talking too much, shut up.

"I wouldn't give you a plumb nickel for it...." — It isn't worth anything.

"He's out to lunch...." — He's stupid.

"He's/she's talking just to hear himself/herself say something." — They are making me sick with their diarrhea of the mouth.

"Who made them/you God?" — A rhetorical question meant to belittle someone's decision or statement

"Come here, and I'll wipe that grin off your face." — Your foolish expression is annoying me, and I would take great pleasure in eradicating it from your face.

"Drop dead." — This is neither rhetorical in some occasions nor is it a request; it is more of a demand.

"I'd just as soon hit him as look at him." — Someone is not simply annoying; he or she is disgusting and genuinely deserves a beating.

"I'll beat you like a rented mule." — Don't tempt me.

"I've forgotten more than you'll ever know…." — This is not a mere practical claim; rather, it is a metaphysical statement, not of simply knowing this or that, but of understanding the nature of the problem, issue, or fact at hand.

"The gift of gab…." — Someone can talk a lot; this could be positive or negative, depending on whether one agreed with or opposed what was being said

"Good grief…." — Signaled "aww" at something said or done, usually from a negative point of view

"I'll knock you into the middle of kingdom come…." — You are really pissing me off, and your time here on Earth is dwindling.

"Talk a blue streak…." — He could really yak in color.

"A petunia in an onion patch…." — You were surrounded by stinkers.

"Good grief…." — The opposite of "bad" grief

"All hell broke loose…." — Chaos with a capital "C"

"You are trying my nerves…." — Quite often, I can tolerate you, but that time has come and gone.

"Going to hell in a hand basket…." — You are doomed, clothed in wicker.

"They were going like a bat out of hell…." — I think it's self-explanatory.

"Go right ahead; we'll come with the next bunch…." — Your driving like a bat out of hell, and you can go right ahead of us.

"We'll end the problem right here and now…." — A problem has come to a head, and it ends now.

"I drank so much I'll have to sleep in the tub tonight…." — Rather than jeopardize life and limb getting up to go to the toilet during the night and during this drunk, you will stay put in the tub and let nature and gravity run its course.

"You are trying my nerves…." — You are getting on my nerves.

"I've forgotten more than you'll ever know…." — I think it's obvious.

"I'm going stark raving mad…." — I'm going "nuckin futs."

"I'll end the problem then and there…." — I'm taking control to settle this or that dispute.

"You're like a bull in a china shop…." — Your physical recklessness is disturbing, so stay away from anything breakable that's mine.

"Would you knock it off…?" — Actually not a request; stop whatever you are doing or saying right now.

"They've got a bit of the devil in them…." — Whoever is in trouble

"I'd like to tap him/her with an ax…." — I'd like to send them to their maker.

"Get over here PDQ…." — Get over here pretty damn quick!

"What in hell do you think you are doing?" — What in hell do you think you are doing?!

"You've got to wake up and die right." — Don't be so stupid